FIRST PAST THE POST®

Mathematics: Worded Problems

Standard Format

Book 2

How to use this book to make the most of 11 plus exam preparation

It is important to remember that for 11 plus exams there is no national syllabus, no pass mark and no retake option. It is therefore vital that your child is fully primed to perform to the best of their ability so that they give themselves the best possible chance on the day.

Mathematics: Worded Problems

This topic-based workbook has been designed to consolidate core 11 plus mathematics knowledge through a series of graded questions: Beginner, Intermediate and Advanced. Each chapter covers a different mathematics topic and comprises 15 questions at each of the difficulty levels. The questions are typical of the mathematics and numerical reasoning sections of the 11 plus and Common Entrance exams. The questions have been designed to be answered without the use of a calculator. Additional paper should be used for any rough working out.

Never has it been more useful to learn from mistakes!

Students can improve by as much as 15%, not only by focused practice, but also by targeting any weak areas.

How to manage your child's practice

To get the most up-to-date information, visit our website, www.elevenplusexams.co.uk, the UK's largest online resource for 11 plus, with over 65,000 webpages and a forum administered by a select group of experienced moderators.

About the authors

The Eleven Plus Exams' **First Past The Post®** series has been created by a team of experienced tutors and authors from leading British universities.

Published by Technical One Ltd t/a Eleven Plus Exams

With special thanks to all the children who tested our material at the ElevenPlusExams centre in Harrow.

ISBN: 978-1-912364-46-6 (previously 978-1-908684-93-6)

Copyright © ElevenPlusExams.co.uk 2017

Second edition

All rights reserved. No part of this publication may be reproduced, stored or introduced into a retrieval system or transmitted in any form or by any means, without the prior written permission of the publisher nor may be circulated in any form of binding or cover other than the one in which it was published and without a similar condition including this condition being imposed on the subsequent publisher.

About Us

At Eleven Plus Exams, we supply high-quality 11 plus tuition for your children. Our free website at **www.elevenplusexams.co.uk** is the largest website in the UK that specifically prepares children for the 11 plus exams. We also provide online services to schools and our **First Past The Post®** range of books has been well-received by schools, tuition centres and parents.

Eleven Plus Exams is recognised as a trusted and authoritative source. We have been quoted in numerous national newspapers, including *The Telegraph*, *The Observer*, the *Daily Mail* and *The Sunday Telegraph*, as well as on national television (BBC1 and Channel 4), and BBC radio.

Our website offers a vast amount of information and advice on the 11 plus, including a moderated online forum, books, downloadable material and online services to enhance your child's chances of success. Set up in 2004, the website grew from an initial 20 webpages to more than 65,000 today, and has been visited by millions of parents. It is moderated by experts in the field, who provide support for parents both before and after the exams.

Don't forget to visit **www.elevenplusexams.co.uk** and see why we are the market's leading one-stop shop for all your 11 plus needs. You will find:

- ✓ Comprehensive quality content and advice written by 11 plus experts
- ✓ Eleven Plus Exams online shop supplying a wide range of practice books, e-papers, software and apps
- ✓ Lots of FREE practice papers to download
- ✓ Professional tuition service
- ✓ Short revision courses
- ✓ Year-long 11 plus courses
- ✓ Mock exams tailored to reflect those of the main examining bodies

Other Titles in the First Past The Post® Series
11+ Essentials Range of Books

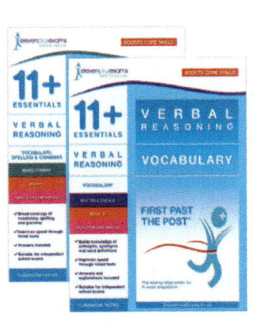

978-1-912364-60-2	Verbal Reasoning: Cloze Tests Book 1 - Mixed Format
978-1-912364-61-9	Verbal Reasoning: Cloze Tests Book 2 - Mixed Format
978-1-912364-78-7	Verbal Reasoning: Cloze Tests Book 3 - Mixed Format
978-1-912364-79-4	Verbal Reasoning: Cloze Tests Book 4 - Mixed Format
978-1-912364-62-6	Verbal Reasoning: Vocabulary Book 1 - Multiple Choice
978-1-912364-63-3	Verbal Reasoning: Vocabulary Book 2 - Multiple Choice
978-1-912364-64-0	Verbal Reasoning: Vocabulary Book 3 - Multiple Choice
978-1-912364-65-7	Verbal Reasoning: Vocabulary, Spelling and Grammar Book 1 - Multiple Choice
978-1-912364-66-4	Verbal Reasoning: Vocabulary, Spelling and Grammar Book 2 - Multiple Choice
978-1-912364-68-8	Verbal Reasoning: Vocabulary in Context Level 1
978-1-912364-69-5	Verbal Reasoning: Vocabulary in Context Level 2
978-1-912364-70-1	Verbal Reasoning: Vocabulary in Context Level 3
978-1-912364-71-8	Verbal Reasoning: Vocabulary in Context Level 4
978-1-912364-74-9	Verbal Reasoning: Vocabulary Puzzles Book 1
978-1-912364-75-6	Verbal Reasoning: Vocabulary Puzzles Book 2
978-1-912364-76-3	Verbal Reasoning: Practice Papers Book 1 - Multiple Choice

978-1-912364-02-2	English: Comprehensions Classic Literature Book 1 - Multiple Choice
978-1-912364-05-3	English: Comprehensions Contemporary Literature Book 1 - Multiple Choice
978-1-912364-08-4	English: Comprehensions Non-Fiction Book 1 - Multiple Choice
978-1-912364-14-5	English: Mini Comprehensions - Inference Book 1
978-1-912364-15-2	English: Mini Comprehensions - Inference Book 2
978-1-912364-16-9	English: Mini Comprehensions - Inference Book 3
978-1-912364-11-4	English: Mini Comprehensions - Fact-Finding Book 1
978-1-912364-12-1	English: Mini Comprehensions - Fact-Finding Book 2
978-1-912364-21-3	English: Spelling, Punctuation and Grammar Book 1
978-1-912364-00-8	English: Practice Papers Book 1 - Multiple Choice
978-1-912364-17-6	Creative Writing Examples

978-1-912364-30-5	Numerical Reasoning: Quick-Fire Book 1
978-1-912364-31-2	Numerical Reasoning: Quick-Fire Book 2
978-1-912364-32-9	Numerical Reasoning: Quick-Fire Book 1 - Multiple Choice
978-1-912364-33-6	Numerical Reasoning: Quick-Fire Book 2 - Multiple Choice
978-1-912364-34-3	Numerical Reasoning: Multi-Part Book 1
978-1-912364-35-0	Numerical Reasoning: Multi-Part Book 2
978-1-912364-36-7	Numerical Reasoning: Multi-Part Book 1 - Multiple Choice
978-1-912364-37-4	Numerical Reasoning: Multi-Part Book 2 - Multiple Choice

978-1-912364-43-5	Mathematics: Mental Arithmetic Book 1
978-1-912364-44-2	Mathematics: Mental Arithmetic Book 2
978-1-912364-45-9	Mathematics: Worded Problems Book 1
978-1-912364-46-6	Mathematics: Worded Problems Book 2
978-1-912364-52-7	Mathematics: Worded Problems Book 3
978-1-912364-47-3	Mathematics: Dictionary Plus
978-1-912364-50-3	Mathematics: Crossword Puzzles Book 1
978-1-912364-51-0	Mathematics: Crossword Puzzles Book 2
978-1-912364-48-0	Mathematics: Practice Papers Book 1 - Multiple Choice

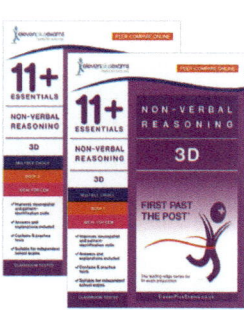

978-1-912364-87-9	Non-Verbal Reasoning: 2D Book 1 - Multiple Choice
978-1-912364-88-6	Non-Verbal Reasoning: 2D Book 2 - Multiple Choice
978-1-912364-85-5	Non-Verbal Reasoning: 3D Book 1 - Multiple Choice
978-1-912364-86-2	Non-Verbal Reasoning: 3D Book 2 - Multiple Choice
978-1-912364-83-1	Non-Verbal Reasoning: Practice Papers Book 1 - Multiple Choice

Contents

Glossary	vi
Instructions	xii
Four Operations	1
Number Values and Number Sequences	5
Factors and Multiples	9
Fractions and Decimals	13
Percentages, Ratios and Proportions	17
Algebra and Number Machines	21
Averages and Representing Data	25
Measures and Reading Scales	29
Dates, Time and Timetables	33
Lines, Angles and Bearings	37
2D Shapes, Perimeters, Areas and Symmetry	41
3D Shapes and Volumes	45
Probability	49
Coordinates and Transformations	53
Answers & Explanations	57

This workbook comprises 14 chapters, each covering a different topic at three different levels of difficulty: Beginner, Intermediate and Advanced. Each chapter comprises 45 questions.

Glossary

Learn the meanings of the terms listed below to expand your mathematical vocabulary.

Apothem - a line segment from the centre of a regular polygon to the midpoint of one of its sides.
Bearing - an angle given in three figures that is measured clockwise from the north direction, e.g. 025°.
BIDMAS - an acronym for **B**rackets, **I**ndices, **D**ivision and **M**ultiplication, and **A**ddition and **S**ubtraction. It is the agreed order of operations used to clarify which should be performed first in a given expression.
Bimodal - when a collection of data has two modes, e.g. in the dataset: {1, 1, 1, 2, 4, 5, 5, 5}, the two modes are 1 and 5.
Bisect - to divide into two equal parts.
Coefficient - a constant that is placed before a variable in an algebraic expression, e.g. in the term $4x$, the coefficient is 4.
Complementary angles - two angles are complementary if they add up to 90°.
Cube number - a number that can be produced by multiplying another number by itself twice, e.g. 8 (= 2 × 2 × 2).
Edge - a line segment that joins two vertices of a 2D shape, or a line segment at which two faces meet in a 3D shape.
Enlargement - a type of transformation in which the size of an object is changed, whilst the ratio of the lengths of its sides stays the same.
Equidistant - two or more points are equidistant if they are the same distance from a common point.
Face - an individual surface of a 3D shape.
Fair - free from bias or equally likely to occur.
Gallon - a unit of volume used for measuring liquids. It is equal to 8 pints, or 4.55 litres.
Gradient - a measure of the steepness of a straight line.
Highest common factor (HCF) - the largest number that is a factor of two or more given numbers, e.g. 5 is the highest common factor of 10 and 15.
Imperial units - the system of units first defined in the British Weights and Measures Act. These units are no longer officially used in Britain, e.g. inches, feet, pints etc.
Inscribe - to draw a shape within another so that their edges touch, but do not intersect.
Integer - a whole number, i.e. not a decimal or a fraction.
Isosceles trapezium - a trapezium with one line of symmetry, two pairs of equal angles and one pair of parallel sides.
Leap year - a calendar year that occurs every four years. It has 366 days, instead of 365, and includes the 29th February. The year 2012 was a leap year.
Lowest common multiple (LCM) - the smallest number that is a multiple of two or more given numbers, e.g. 6 is the lowest common multiple of 2 and 3.
Metric units - a system of units based on multiples of 10, e.g. millimetre (mm), centimetre (cm) or metre (m).
Net - a 2D pattern that can be cut out and folded to make a 3D shape.
Parallel - lines that run side-by-side, always remain the same distance apart and never intersect, even if they are extended.
Perimeter - the total distance around the outside of a 2D shape.
Perpendicular - two lines are perpendicular if they are at an angle of 90° to each other.
Polygon - a 2D shape with three or more straight sides and no curved sides, e.g. triangle, pentagon, hexagon.
Polyhedron - a 3D shape whose faces are polygons, e.g. triangular pyramid, octahedron.
Prime factor - one of a collection of prime numbers whose product is a particular number, i.e. 2 × 2 × 3 = 12, so 2, 2 and 3 are the prime factors of 12.
Prime number - an integer greater than 1 that has no factors other than 1 and itself, e.g. 2, 3, 5.
Prism - a solid 3D shape with two identical, parallel end faces that are connected by flat sides.
Pyramid - a solid 3D shape whose base is a polygon and has triangular faces that meet at a single vertex.
Quadrilateral - a 2D shape with four straight sides. Quadrilaterals are polygons.
Reflective symmetry - a shape or an object has reflective symmetry if an imaginary line can be drawn that divides the shape into two, so that one half is a reflection of the other in the imaginary line.
Regular - a regular polygon has sides of equal length.
Remainder - a number that is left over after a division.
Rotational symmetry - a shape or an object has rotational symmetry if it can be rotated, but still appears to be in the same original position, e.g. a square has rotational symmetry of four, because it can be rotated four times, but still appears the same.
Scalene - the sides of a scalene triangle are all of different lengths.
Sequence - a list of numbers or objects arranged in a particular order, which is defined by a specific rule, or set of rules.
Square number - a number that can be produced by multiplying another number by itself, e.g. 16 (= 4 × 4).
Supplementary angles - two angles are supplementary if they add up to 180°.
Triangle - a 2D shape with three straight sides. Triangles are polygons.
Triangular number - a number that can be represented by a group of equally spaced points arranged in a triangle, e.g. 1, 3, 6: ● ∴ ∴·
Vertex - a point at which two or more straight lines meet.

Place Value

The numerical value of a digit in a number.

For example, in the number 1234.567, the digit 3 has a place value of tens.

1	2	3	4	.	5	6	7
thousands	hundreds	tens	units	decimal point	tenths	hundredths	thousandths

Special Numbers

	1st	2nd	3rd	4th	5th	6th	7th	8th	9th	10th	11th	12th	13th	14th	15th	16th	17th	18th	19th	20th
even	2	4	6	8	10	12	14	16	18	20	22	24	26	28	30	32	34	36	38	40
odd	1	3	5	7	9	11	13	15	17	19	21	23	25	27	29	31	33	35	37	39
square	1	4	9	16	25	36	49	64	81	100	121	144	169	196	225	256	289	324	361	400
cube	1	8	27	64	125	216	343	512	729	1000	1331	1728	2197	2744	3375	4096	4913	5832	6859	8000
triangular	1	3	6	10	15	21	28	36	45	55	66	78	91	105	120	136	153	171	190	210
prime	2	3	5	7	11	13	17	19	23	29	31	37	41	43	47	53	59	61	67	71
fibonacci	1	1	2	3	5	8	13	21	34	55	89	144	233	377	610	987	1597	2584	4181	6765

Equivalent Decimals, Fractions & Percentages

percentage	5%	10%	15%	20%	25%	30%	35%	40%	45%	50%	55%	60%	65%	70%	75%	80%	85%	90%	95%	100%	150%
fraction	$1/20$	$1/10$	$3/20$	$1/5$	$1/4$	$3/10$	$7/20$	$2/5$	$9/20$	$1/2$	$11/20$	$3/5$	$13/20$	$7/10$	$3/4$	$4/5$	$17/20$	$9/10$	$19/20$	$1/1$	$3/2$
decimal	0.05	0.1	0.15	0.2	0.25	0.3	0.35	0.4	0.45	0.5	0.55	0.6	0.65	0.7	0.75	0.8	0.85	0.9	0.95	1	1.5

Mathematical Symbols

+	addition
−	subtraction
×	multiplication
÷	division
±	positive or negative
=	equals sign
<	less than
>	greater than
≈	approximately equal to
≤	less than or equal to
≥	greater than or equal to
≠	not equal to
a^2	squared number
a^3	cubed number
%	per cent
$\sqrt{a}$	square root
$\sqrt[3]{a}$	cubed root
$\dot{a}$	recurring number
$a:b$	ratio
$a°$	degrees
$\bar{a}$	mean
(x, y)	coordinates
∟	right angle
$\binom{x}{y}$	column vector (column matrix)
a/b	fraction
$\{a, b\}$	dataset
π	pi

Equivalent Periods of Time

1 minute	60 seconds
1 hour	60 minutes
1 day	24 hours
1 week	7 days
1 year	12 months (365 days)
1 leap year	366 days
1 decade	10 years
1 century	100 years
1 millennium	1,000 years

Roman Numerals

When a symbol appears *after* a numerically larger symbol, their values are added. When a symbol appears *before* a numerically larger symbol, their values are subtracted.

1	I
2	II
3	III
4	IV
5	V
6	VI
7	VII
8	VIII
9	IX
10	X
20	XX
30	XXX
40	XL
50	L
60	LX
70	LXX
80	LXXX
90	XC
100	C
200	CC
300	CCC
400	CD
500	D
1,000	M

Time Conversion

24-hour clock	12-hour clock
00:00	12.00am
01:00	1.00am
02:00	2.00am
03:00	3.00am
04:00	4.00am
05:00	5.00am
06:00	6.00am
07:00	7.00am
08:00	8.00am
09:00	9.00am
10:00	10.00am
11:00	11.00am
12:00	12.00pm
13:00	1.00pm
14:00	2.00pm
15:00	3.00pm
16:00	4.00pm
17:00	5.00pm
18:00	6.00pm
19:00	7.00pm
20:00	8.00pm
21:00	9.00pm
22:00	10.00pm
23:00	11.00pm

Units of Measurement

	Metric system		Imperial system		
	Units	Conversion	Units	Conversion	Metric approximation
Mass	milligram (mg)	1mg = 0.1cg = 0.001g	ounce (oz)	1oz = $^{1}/_{16}$ lb	1oz ≈ 28g
	centigram (cg)	1cg = 10mg = 0.01g	pound (lb)	1lb = 16oz	1lb ≈ 0.45kg
	gram (g)	1g = 100cg = 0.001kg	stone (st)	1st = 14lb	1st ≈ 6kg
	kilogram (kg)	1kg = 1,000g = 0.001t			
	tonne (t)	1t = 1,000,000g = 1,000kg	ton	1 ton = 160st	1 ton ≈ 0.91 tonne
Length	millimetre (mm)	1mm = 0.1cm = 0.001m	inch (in or ")	1in = $^{1}/_{12}$ ft	1in ≈ 25mm
	centimetre (cm)	1cm = 10mm = 0.01m	foot (ft or ')	1ft = 12in	1ft ≈ 30cm
	metre (m)	1m = 100cm = 0.001km	yard (yd)	1yd = 3ft	1yd ≈ 91cm
	kilometre (km)	1km = 100,000cm = 1,000m	mile	1 mile = 1,760yd	1 mile ≈ 1.6km
Volume	millilitre (ml)	1ml = 0.1cl = 0.001l = 1cm^3	fluid ounce (fl. oz)	1fl. oz = $^{1}/_{20}$ pt	1fl. oz ≈ 28ml
	centilitre (cl)	1cl = 10ml = 0.01l = 10cm^3	pint (pt)	1pt = 20fl. oz	1pt ≈ 0.57l
	litre (l)	1l = 100cl = 0.001kl = 1,000cm^3			
	kilolitre (kl)	1kl = 1,000l = 1,000,000cm^3	gallon (gal)	1gal = 8pt	1gal ≈ 4.5l

Types of Angles

Zero angle
Equivalent to 0°
The angle AÔB is an example of a zero angle.

Acute angle
An angle greater than 0°, but smaller than 90°
Angle $c°$ (AÔB) is an example of an acute angle.

Right angle
An angle of 90°
Angle $d°$ (AÔB) is an example of a right angle.

Obtuse angle
An angle greater than 90°, but smaller than 180°
Angle $e°$ (AÔB) is an example of an obtuse angle.

Flat angle
An angle of 180°
The angle AÔB is an example of a flat angle.

Reflex angle
An angle greater than 180°, but smaller than 360°
Angle $f°$ (AÔB) is an example of a reflex angle.

Full rotation
A full turn, equal to 360°

Pairs of Angles

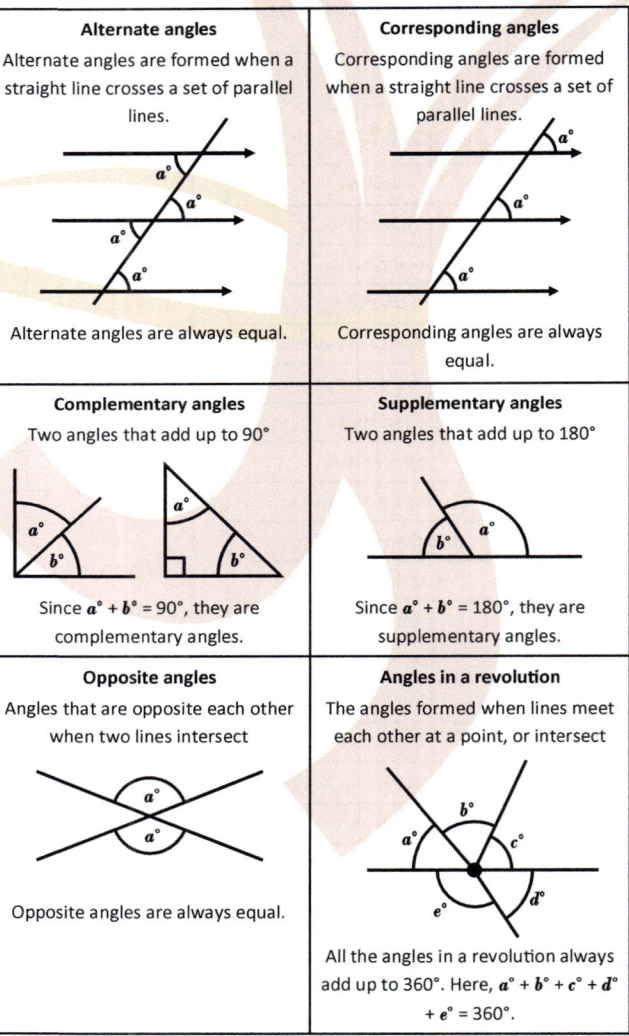

Alternate angles
Alternate angles are formed when a straight line crosses a set of parallel lines.
Alternate angles are always equal.

Corresponding angles
Corresponding angles are formed when a straight line crosses a set of parallel lines.
Corresponding angles are always equal.

Complementary angles
Two angles that add up to 90°
Since $a° + b° = 90°$, they are complementary angles.

Supplementary angles
Two angles that add up to 180°
Since $a° + b° = 180°$, they are supplementary angles.

Opposite angles
Angles that are opposite each other when two lines intersect
Opposite angles are always equal.

Angles in a revolution
The angles formed when lines meet each other at a point, or intersect
All the angles in a revolution always add up to 360°. Here, $a° + b° + c° + d° + e° = 360°$.

2D Shapes

Figures with two dimensions: length and width.

Circle	Right-angled triangle	Equilateral triangle	Isosceles triangle	Scalene triangle
r = radius d = diameter. The perimeter of a circle is its circumference.	One angle is a right angle (90°). The other two angles are complementary.	All three angles are equal (60°). All three sides are of equal length.	Two angles are equal. Two sides are of equal length.	No angles are equal. No sides are of equal length.

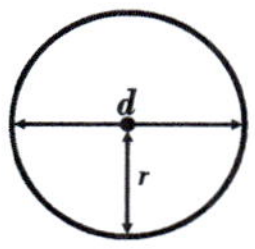

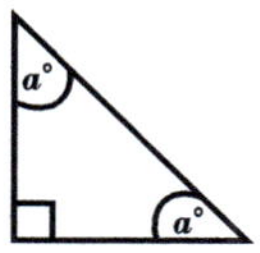

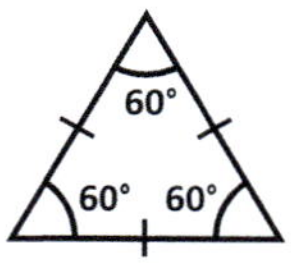

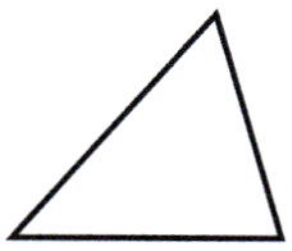

Square	Trapezium	Rhombus	Parallelogram	Kite
All four angles are equal (90°). All four sides are of equal length. The diagonals bisect each other at 90°.	One pair of opposite sides is parallel.	Opposite angles are equal. All sides are of equal length. The diagonals bisect each other at 90°.	Opposite angles are equal. Opposite sides are parallel and of equal length. The diagonals bisect each other.	Two of the opposite angles are equal. Two pairs of sides are of equal lengths. The diagonals intersect at 90°.

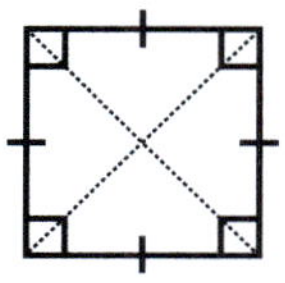

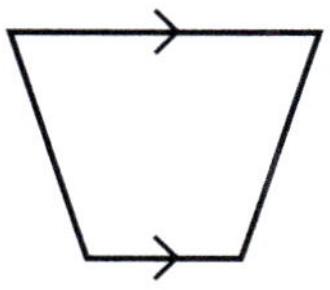

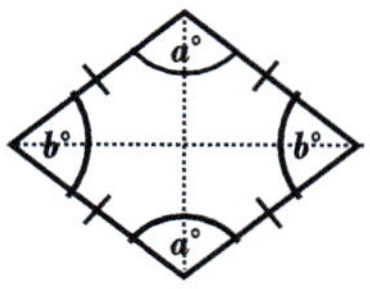

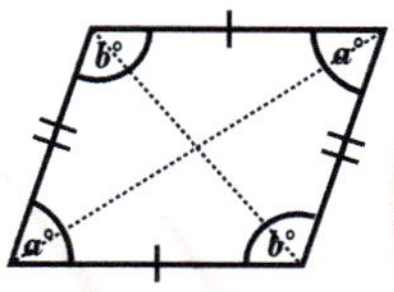

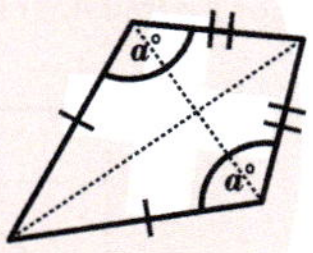

Regular pentagon	Regular hexagon	Regular heptagon	Regular octagon	Regular nonagon
All five angles are equal. All five sides are of equal length. The sum of the interior angles is 540°.	All six angles are equal. All six sides are of equal length. The sum of the interior angles is 720°.	All seven angles are equal. All seven sides are of equal length. The sum of the interior angles is 900°.	All eight angles are equal. All eight sides are of equal length. The sum of the interior angles is 1,080°.	All nine angles are equal. All nine sides are of equal length. The sum of the interior angles is 1,260°.

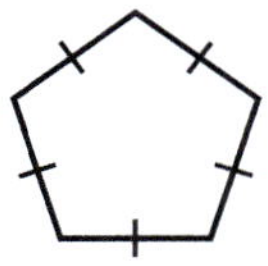

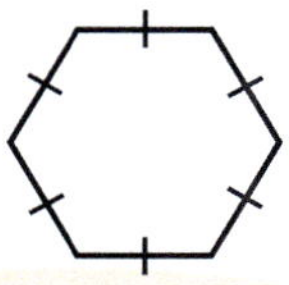

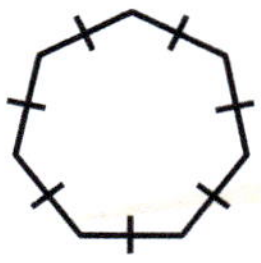

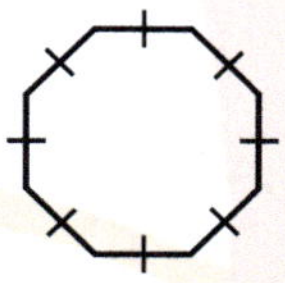

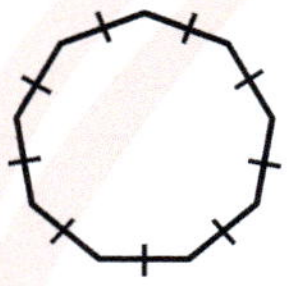

3D Shapes

Figures with three dimensions: length, width and depth.

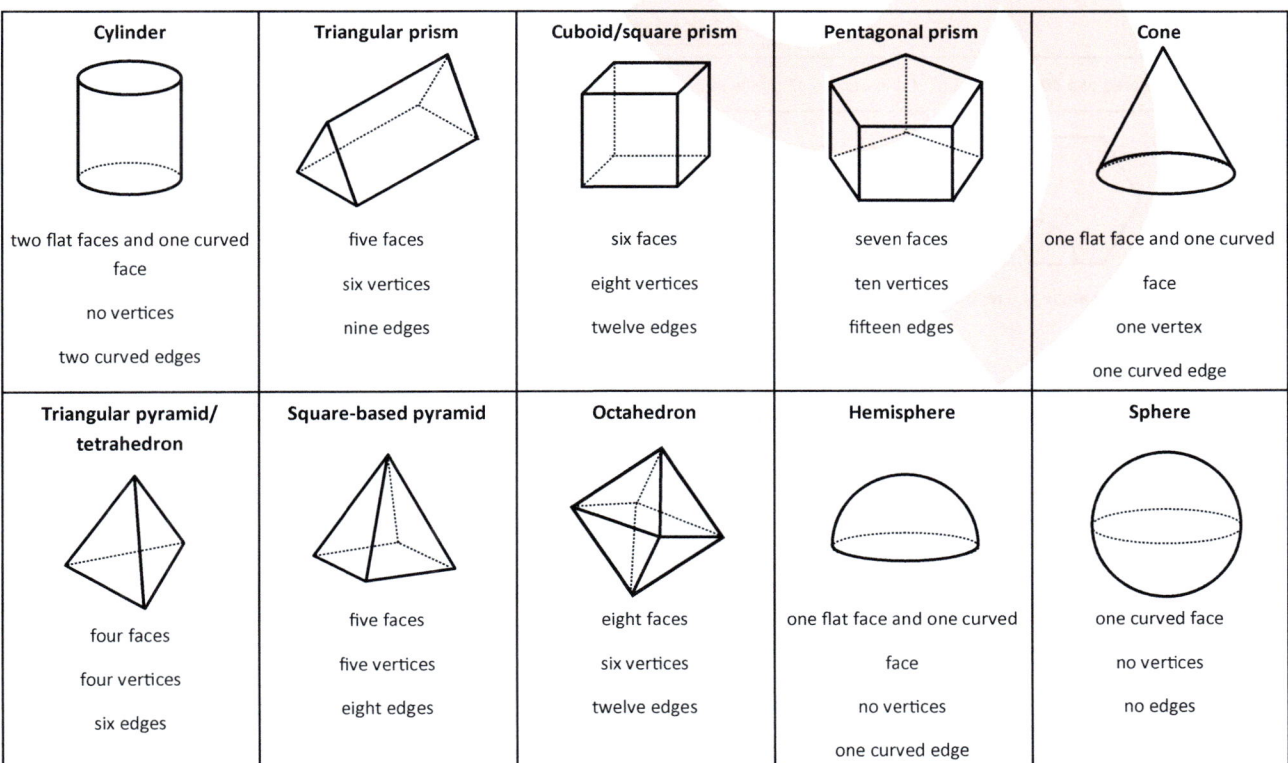

Cylinder	Triangular prism	Cuboid/square prism	Pentagonal prism	Cone
two flat faces and one curved face; no vertices; two curved edges	five faces; six vertices; nine edges	six faces; eight vertices; twelve edges	seven faces; ten vertices; fifteen edges	one flat face and one curved face; one vertex; one curved edge

Triangular pyramid/ tetrahedron	Square-based pyramid	Octahedron	Hemisphere	Sphere
four faces; four vertices; six edges	five faces; five vertices; eight edges	eight faces; six vertices; twelve edges	one flat face and one curved face; no vertices; one curved edge	one curved face; no vertices; no edges

Area Formulae

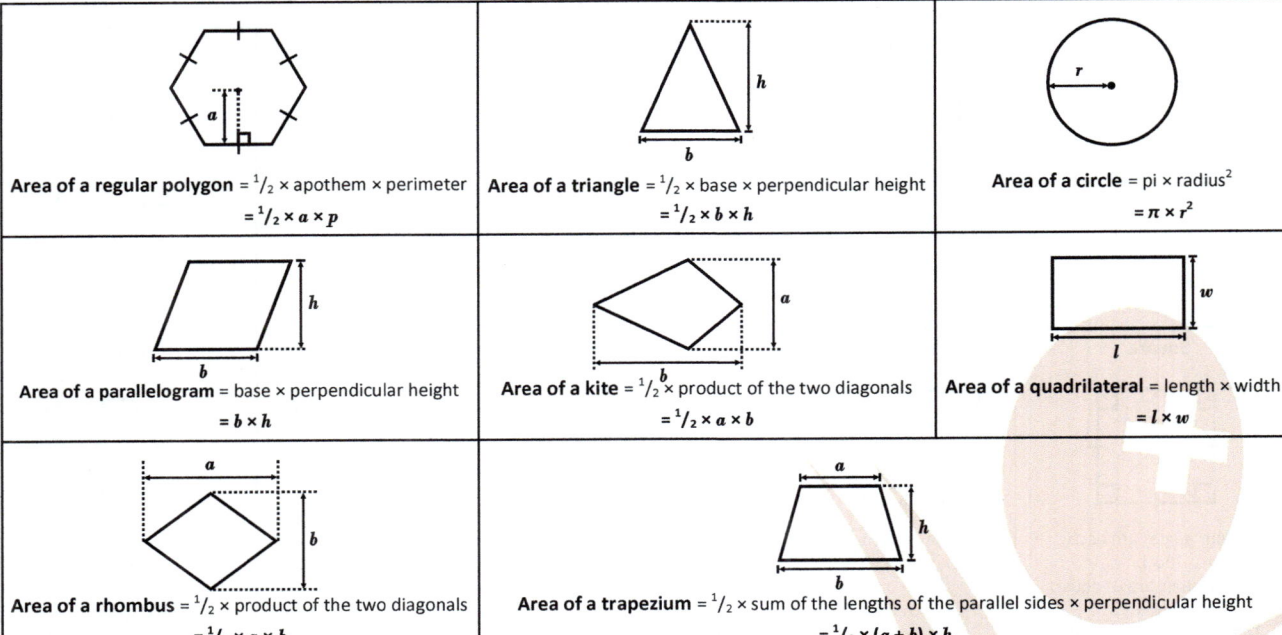

Volume Formulae

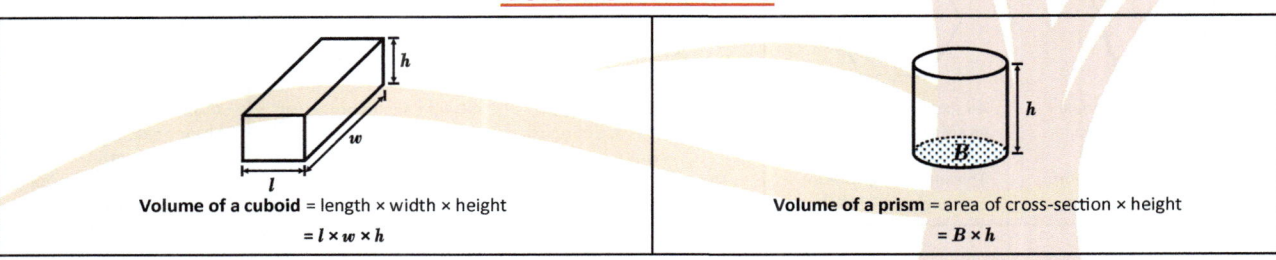

Other Useful Formulae

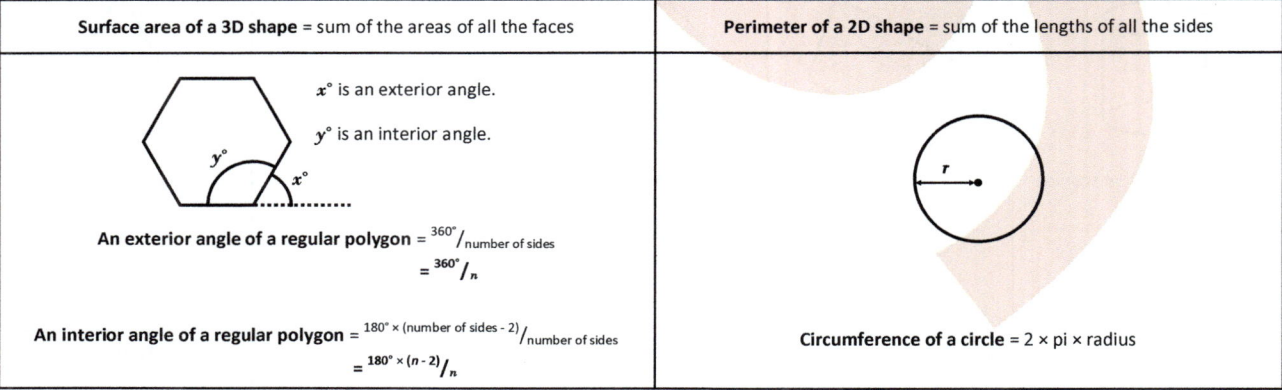

Probability

A measure of how likely it is that a particular event will occur.

The probability of event A happening, P(A), is given by: number of ways in which event A can happen ÷ total number of possible outcomes.

'And' rule

The 'and' rule is used to find the probability of a combination of events occurring.

The probability of events A **and** B happening is:
$$P(A \text{ and } B) = P(A) \times P(B)$$

'Or' rule

The 'or' rule is used to find the probability of one or other event occurring.

The probability of event A **or** B happening is:
$$P(A \text{ or } B) = P(A) + P(B)$$

The word 'or' is replaced by an addition sign.

Tree diagram

One way of illustrating the probabilities of different events occurring is by using branches on a tree diagram. Each branch represents one possible event and is labelled with its probability.

e.g. a tree diagram illustrating two tosses of an unbiased coin

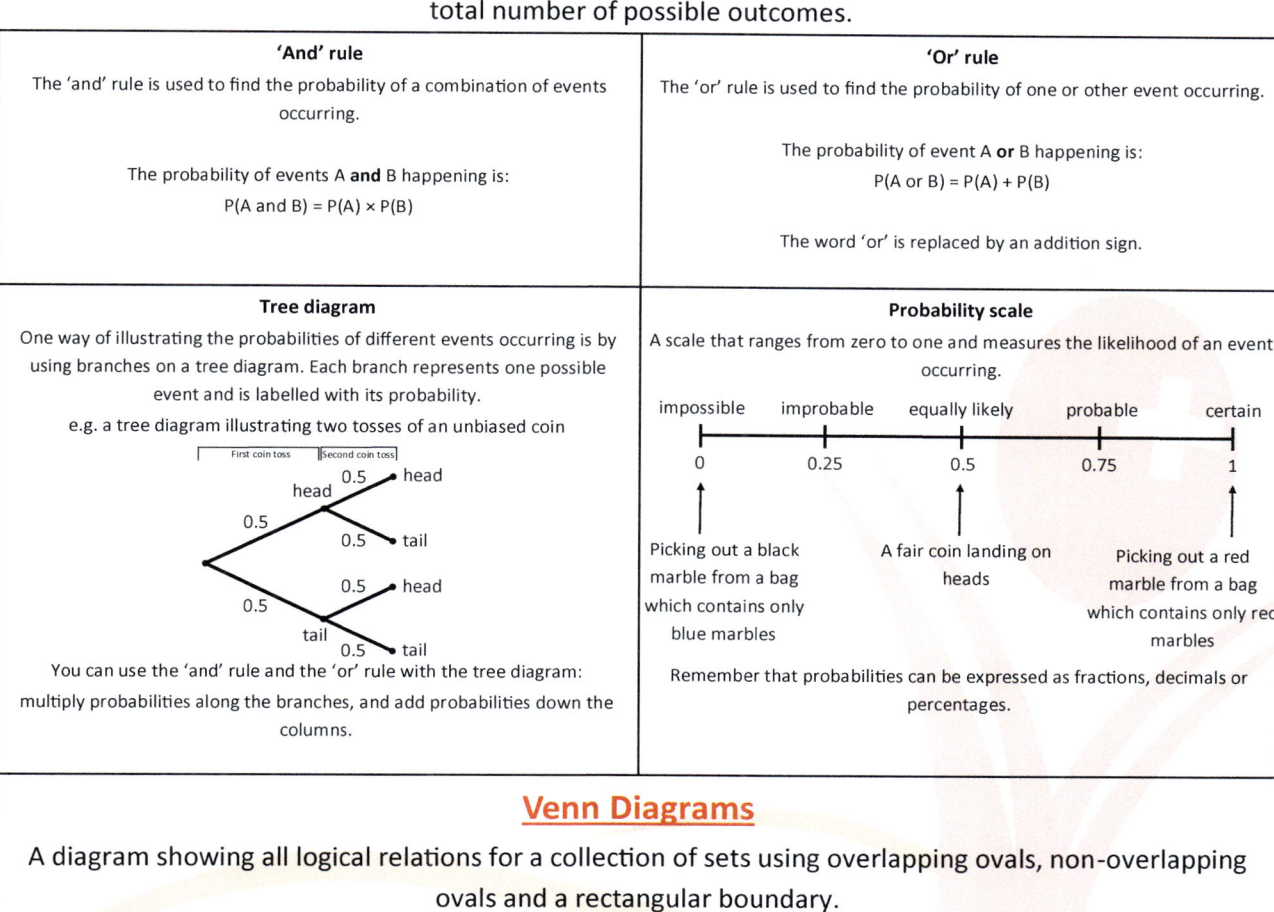

You can use the 'and' rule and the 'or' rule with the tree diagram: multiply probabilities along the branches, and add probabilities down the columns.

Probability scale

A scale that ranges from zero to one and measures the likelihood of an event occurring.

impossible — improbable — equally likely — probable — certain
0 — 0.25 — 0.5 — 0.75 — 1

Picking out a black marble from a bag which contains only blue marbles

A fair coin landing on heads

Picking out a red marble from a bag which contains only red marbles

Remember that probabilities can be expressed as fractions, decimals or percentages.

Venn Diagrams

A diagram showing all logical relations for a collection of sets using overlapping ovals, non-overlapping ovals and a rectangular boundary.

e.g. a Venn diagram showing the first ten positive integers

The oval represents a set. A set is a collection of numbers that share a particular property. In this case, it is a set of triangular numbers.

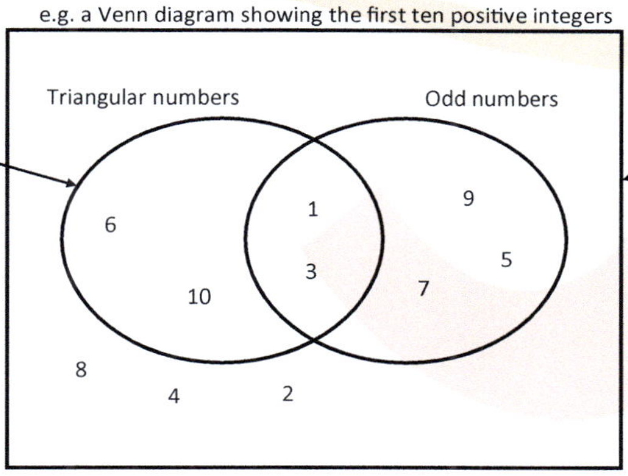

Triangular numbers: 6, 10, 8, 4
Intersection: 1, 3
Odd numbers: 9, 5, 7
Outside: 2

The rectangle represents the universal set. The universal set contains all the elements in the sets within it. In this case, it is the set of the first ten positive integers.

Useful Venn diagram patterns:

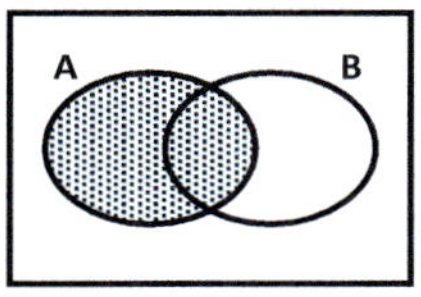

- set **A**
- set **B** 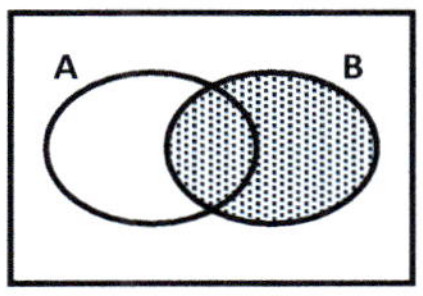
- not **A** 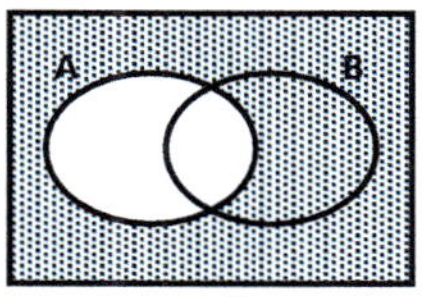
- not **B** 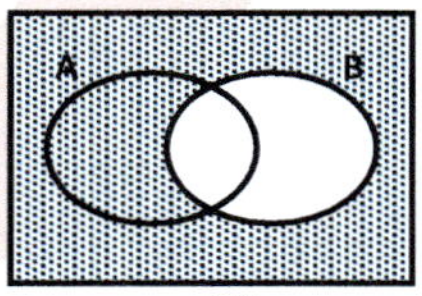
- **A** or **B** 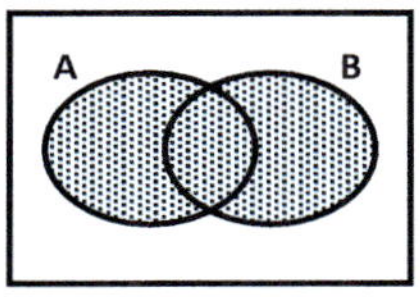
- **A** and **B** 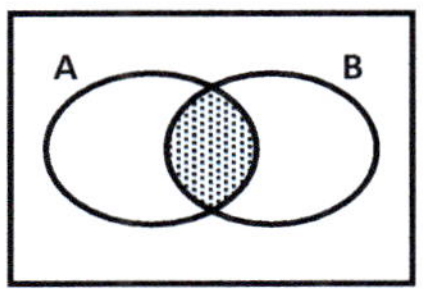
- only **A** or only **B** 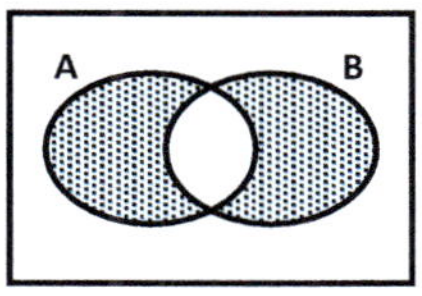
- not **A** and not **B**

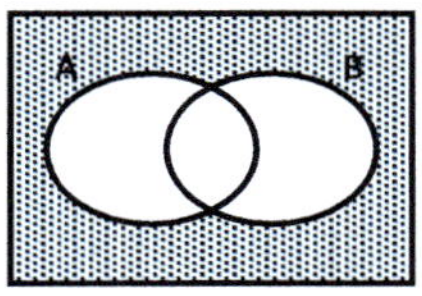

Instructions

Answer lines are provided on which to write your answers.

Write your answers on the answer lines provided as shown below:

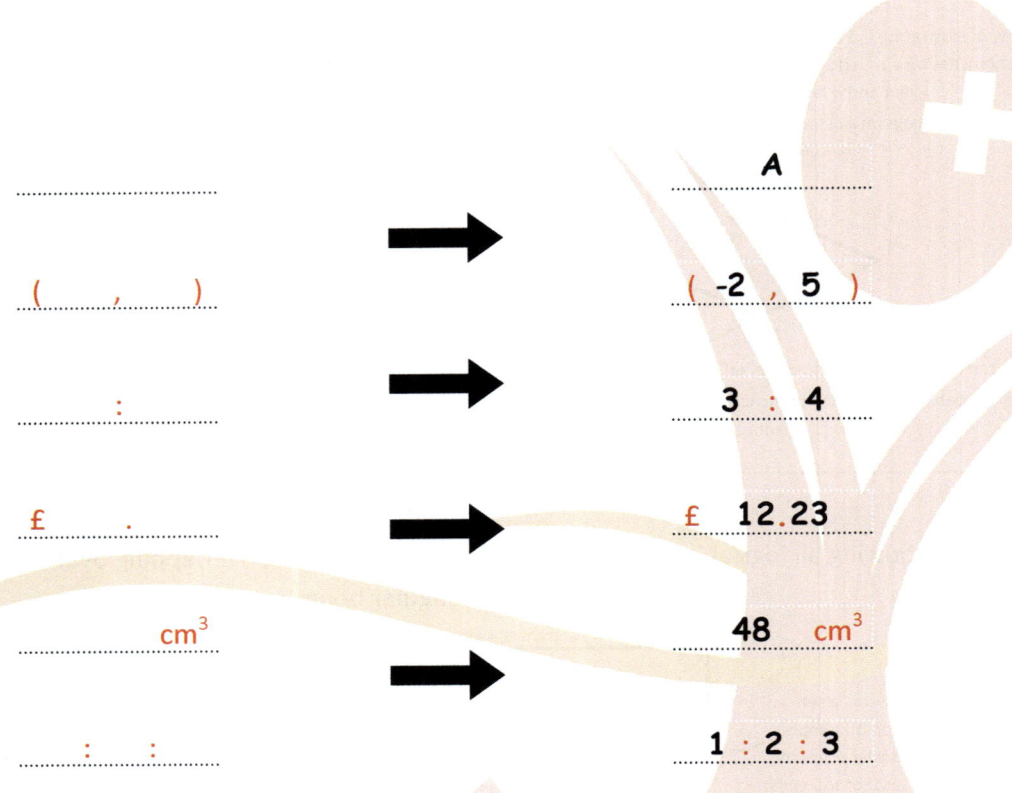

Four Operations

Four Operations - Beginner

1. A small mobile library has 267 books on its shelves. It also has a further 55 books out on loan. How many books has the library got altogether?

2. What is the difference between 838 and 383?

3. In the grid below, the three numbers in each row and in each column, when added, equal 24. What number should replace the question mark?

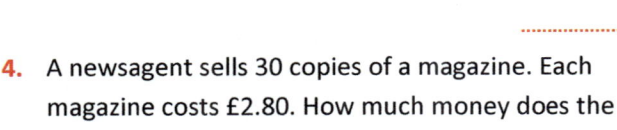

4. A newsagent sells 30 copies of a magazine. Each magazine costs £2.80. How much money does the newsagent receive for the sale?

   £ ....

5. A garden centre has 20 identically priced lawnmowers for sale at a total cost of £2,700. What is the total cost of three of the lawnmowers?

   £ ....

6. If B = 9, what is the value of A in the equation below?

   $(A \times A) + (B \times B) = 130$

7. Ali thinks of a number N. He multiplies N by 100 and then divides the result by 60. If Ali's final answer is 30, what is the value of N?

8. In the number pyramid below, the number in each box is equal to the product of the numbers in the two boxes below it. What number should be entered in the top box?

9. A 10p coin weighs 6.5g. What is the weight of a bag of 10p coins worth £3.60?

   .... g

10. There are 10 bottles of water in a pack and 100 packs in a crate. If there is 65,000ml of water in the crate, what is the quantity of water in one bottle?

    .... ml

11. Use the rules of combined operations to work out the result of:

    $83 - 8 \times 7 + 91$

12. Using the information on the diagram below, work out the perimeter of the carpet.

    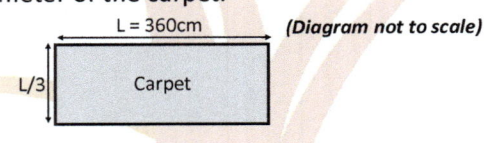

    .... cm

13. In the equation below, the same single digit number must be placed in both boxes to balance the equation. What is the missing number?

    $15 \times \boxed{?} - 3 = 12 \times \boxed{?} + 24$

14. Jane has a total of 240 different coloured counters in a bag. One third are red and one eighth of the remaining counters are blue. How many counters in the bag are neither red nor blue?

15. Use the rules of combined operations to work out the result of:

    $(72 - 16) \div 8 + 5 \times 9$

Four Operations - Intermediate

1. Seven 462mm strips are cut from a 3.24m length of plastic capping. What length of capping is left over? Express your answer in cm.

   .... cm

2. Both positive and negative numbers are used in the number grid below. The sum of each row and each column is the same. What are the missing numbers represented by R and S?

-7	10	1
R		S
3	-5	

   R = ... , S = ...

3. What is the perimeter of the shaded inset area of the picture frame below? Express your answer in mm.

   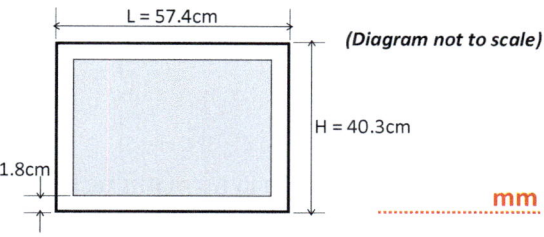

   .... mm

4. A number *N* is multiplied by 65 and 7 is subtracted from the result. Finally, dividing by 4 results in an answer of 47. What is number *N*?

   ....

5. Mia purchases 8 CDs each costing £6.35 and six marker pens priced at 85p for two. How much does Mia pay altogether?

   £..................

6. In the number pyramid below, the number in each box is equal to the product of the numbers in the two boxes below it. What number should be entered in the top box?

   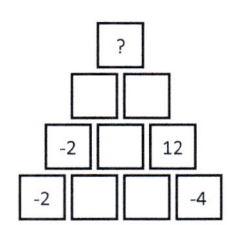

   ....

7. 2,526 people attend a theatre performance. One third sit upstairs and the remainder sit downstairs. Three quarters of those downstairs are adults. How many children are downstairs?

   ....

8. Omar throws three darts at a dart board and scores a single 17, a double 18 and a treble 19. He then subtracts his score from his starting number of 501. What number is left?

   ....

9. What is the difference between five eighths of 48 and two thirds of 48?

   ....

10. Mr Smith buys a car priced at £8,560. The garage agrees to take off $^1/_{16}$ of the sale price as Mr Smith requires a £521 Satellite Navigation and a £940 Parking Assist installed as extras. How much does Mr Smith pay for the car and extras in total?

    £..................

11. Use the rules of combined operations to work out the result of:

    $$(81 + (-9)) \times 2 + 30007$$

    ....

12. The unknown value C is common to both of the equations shown below. What is the answer R in equation 1?

    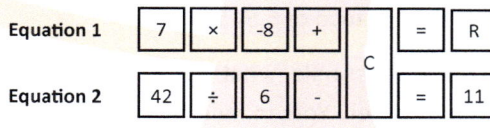

    ....

13. Using the equations below, what is the result of A ÷ B?

    $$A = 17 + (8 \times 3) - 3 \qquad B = -8 + (21 \div 7) + 3$$

    ....

14. Mrs Davis is offered two methods of payment for the purchase of a £360 dishwasher. Method 1: pay £360 cash, method 2: pay a deposit of £42 and 24 monthly payments of £14.40. What is the difference in cost between the two methods of payment?

    £..................

15. Find the answer to the expression below.

    $$-12 + (4 \times 7) - (-4) + (18 \div 6) + (-9)$$

    ....

Four Operations - Advanced

1. A supermarket has a one-day special offer: 'For every £10 spent, get 75p off'. Fabia purchases five items costing £12.35, £7.50, £10.72, £16.93 and £4.67. How much does Fabia pay in total?

   £ ....

Both positive and negative numbers are used in the number grid below. The sum of each row and each column is the same. Using this information, answer questions 2 to 4.

P	-6	7
Q	R	S
3.6	-6.2	-5.4

2. What are the missing values P and Q?

   P = ... , Q = ...

3. What is the missing value R?

   R = ...

4. What is the missing value S?

   S = ...

5. An aircraft leaves London at 12:30pm London time and arrives in New York at 3.30pm New York time, with a flight distance of 5,545km.

   (a) To the nearest mile, what is the distance from London to New York in miles? (Use 1 mile ≈ 1.61km)

   (b) If London time is 5 hours ahead of New York time, what was the actual flight time in hours?

   (a) .... miles, (b) .... hrs

6. Insert an extra pair of brackets in the expression below to create an overall answer of 2.

   7.5 - (-12) - 3.5 × 4 + 1

7. In the number pyramid below, the number in each box is equal to the product of the numbers in the two boxes below it. What number should be entered in the top box, to 2 decimal places?

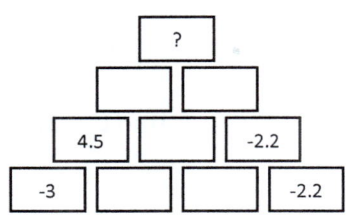

8. Work out the result of the expression below.

   (-48 ÷ (-4 + (-0.4) - 3.6) - 3^3 + 5 × 5.2) ÷ 2.5

   ....

9. Find the:
   (a) perimeter of the whole shape
   (b) area of the isosceles triangle (T)

   L = 18cm, W = L/3, 5cm, 22cm *(Diagram not to scale)*

   (a) .... cm, (b) .... cm^2

10. Lara multiplies the seventh square number by the sixth prime number. She then subtracts the seventh triangular number from the sixth cube number. Lara finally divides her first result by her second result and rounds the answer to the nearest tenth. What is Lara's final answer?

    ....

11. Sean made a mistake in his maths test. He divided a number N by 9 instead of multiplying it by 9. His answer was 8,167. What should Sean's answer have been?

    ....

12. Kim is reading a novel containing 364 pages of text. She has read $4/7$ of the pages in the book. How many more pages must Kim read to reach $6/7$ of the way through the book?

    ....

13. Planks of wood are sold in lengths of 3,580mm. Okello requires 13 planks of wood each 119cm long and 9 planks each 160cm long. What is the minimum number of 3,580mm planks Okello must purchase?

    ....

14. Seventeen pizzas were each cut into eighths ready for sale at 72p a slice. At the end of the day, the pizza outlet had sold £82.80 worth of pizza slices. How many pizzas were left unsold expressed in decimal number format?

    ....

15. Tanya weighs 10 stone. Her car weighs 1.25 metric tonnes. If 1 stone ≈ 6.35kg, what is the total weight of the car and Tanya to the nearest kg?

    .... kg

Number Values and Sequences

Number Values and Number Sequences - Beginner

1. The distance from London to New York is three thousand four hundred and fifty-nine miles. Express this number of miles in figures.

   ....

2. The height of a block of flats is 24,615cm. Express the number 24,615 in words.

   ....

3. Write the set of numbers below in descending order.

   77,807   78,387   77,838   78,738   77,883

   ....

4. The quantity of water in container one is 20,007ml and the quantity in container two is two thousand and seven millilitres. What is the difference between the two quantities?

   .... ml

5. A washing machine costs £384.50. In the price, how many pounds (£) is the 8 worth?

   £ ....

6. What is the value of N in the breakdown of the number 14,327 below?

   14327 = 10000 + $\boxed{N}$ + 300 + 20 + 7

   ....

7. Kim's laptop weighs 10.63kg. What is this weight to the nearest kg?

   .... kg

8. How many thousands equal 160 hundreds?

   ....

9. Each small square below is made up of four matchsticks. How many matchsticks are needed to create pattern six in the sequence?

   Pattern 1   Pattern 2   Pattern 3

   ....

10. The rule for finding the nth term in a sequence is $7n$. What is the sum of the third and fifth terms?

    ....

11. What is the rule for finding the nth pattern of circles in the sequence below?

    Pattern 1   Pattern 2   Pattern 3

    ....

12. What is the missing number in the sequence below?

    −8   ?   8   16   24   32   40

    ....

13. The rule for finding the nth term in the sequence below is in the form of $n + ?$. Write down the full rule for the nth term.

8	9	10	11	12
Term 1	Term 2	Term 3	Term 4	Term 5

    ....

14. How many circles in total are needed to create patterns six and eight in the sequence below?

    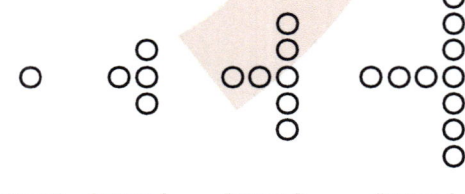

    Pattern 1   Pattern 2   Pattern 3   Pattern 4

    ....

15. What is the sum of the missing terms A and B in the sequence below?

    A   4.02   4.05   4.08   B

    ....

Number Values and Number Sequences - Intermediate

1. What is the number 734,601 expressed in words?

2. An Olympic-sized swimming pool contains three million two thousand three hundred and seventy-four litres of water. Write this quantity of water in number format.

3. What is the difference between the second and fifth largest numbers in the set of numbers below?

   219,807   227,207   220,782   227,028
   218,728   227,802   218,782

4. Farida writes down the worth of each underlined digit in the numbers below. She then adds together her three results. What is Farida's final answer?

   47286   9138   654279

5. Television A costs £196.27 and television B costs £298.74. The cost of television A is rounded to the nearest £10 and the cost of television B is rounded to the nearest pound (£). What is the sum of the rounded costs of both televisions?

   £ ....

6. Write the number 403.2095 correct to three decimal places (3dp).

7. The price of a diamond ring is 10,000 times that of a cheap ring priced at £1.54. What is the price of the diamond ring rounded to the nearest £1000?

   £ ....

8. The patterns of rectangles below represent a common sequence of numbers. How many rectangles in total are required to create patterns seven, eight and nine?

9. What is the rule for finding the nth term in the sequence of numbers below?

   7   12   17   22   27

10. The nth term rule for a sequence of numbers is $3n - 2$. What is the result of subtracting the fourth term from the seventh term?

11. What is the value of the missing term in the sequence below expressed as a mixed number?

    $1\frac{1}{8}$ $2\frac{1}{4}$ $3\frac{3}{8}$ $4\frac{1}{2}$? $6\frac{3}{4}$

12. The diagram below shows a repeating pattern of shaded and unshaded hexagons. Will the 38th hexagon be shaded or unshaded?

13. In a descending number sequence, dividing a term by three gives the value of the next term. If the sixth term is three, what is the value of the second term?

14. What are the missing terms A and B in the sequence below?

    2   1   4   3   6   6   8   10   10   A   B

    A = ... , B = ...

15. John rounds each of the six numbers below to the nearest 10 and then creates an ascending number sequence with the rounded results. Write down John's ascending rounded number sequence.

    54.85   26.18   35.63   18.71   10.42   57.24

Number Values and Number Sequences - Advanced

1. (a) Write the numbers in the set below in descending order of size.

   5,553,053   5,335,335   5,535,335

   5,535,355   5,553,353   5,535,053

   ....

   (b) What is the difference between the second and fourth largest numbers in the set?

   ....

2. The distance from Earth to the planet Mercury is 56,974,146 miles. What is the distance between the two planets to the nearest 100,000 miles?

   ....

3. Write down the value of each of the underlined digits in the numbers below.

   7<u>6</u>84321,   8<u>3</u>029705,   <u>2</u>15408396

   ...., ..., ...

4. Three similar passenger-carrying hot-air balloons hold one million seven hundred and forty-three thousand eight hundred and four cubic feet of air in total.

   (a) Write down this value in numerical form.

   .... cubic feet

   (b) How much air does one balloon hold to the nearest 100 cubic feet?

   .... cubic feet

5. (a) Write the number 2048.7169 to three decimal places and write the number 1700.054 to two decimal places.

   .... to 3dp, ... to 2dp

   (b) Add together the two results obtained in Q5(a) and round the answer to the nearest hundredth.

   ....

6. If 1 billion = 1000 million and 1 trillion = 1000 billion, what is 10 trillion divided by five million?

   ....

7. A large delivery company delivers 17,846,529 parcels in one year. If the number of parcels is rounded to the nearest 10,000, what is the difference between the actual and rounded numbers of parcels?

8. In the sequence of patterns below, how many circles are needed to create the 32nd pattern?

   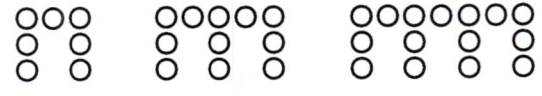

   Pattern 1   Pattern 2   Pattern 3

   ....

9. Referring to the pattern sequence in Q8 above, which pattern number has 219 circles?

   ....

10. What are the values of the two missing terms A and B in the sequence below?

    1 A 4 3 9 6 16 10 B 15 36 21

    A = ... , B = ...

11. The nth term of a sequence is $3.5 - 5n/4$. Write down the first four terms.

    .... , ... , ... , ...

12. Write down the rule for the number of small circles in the pattern sequence below. Express your answer in terms of pattern n.

    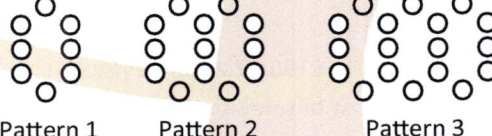

    Pattern 1   Pattern 2   Pattern 3

    ....

13. Look at the repeating pattern of squares below. Which capital letter will be on the 94th square?

    ....

14. Write down the rule for the nth term of the sequence below.

    20   15   10   5   0   -5

    ....

15. Rewrite each of the six numbers below to one decimal place (1dp) of accuracy and then list them in descending order to form a sequence.

    46.39   50.88   55.41   41.92   37.37   32.86

    .... , ... , ... , ... , ... , ...

Factors and Multiples

Factors and Multiples - Beginner

1. How many factors does the number 12 have?

2. What number between one and 10 has only two factors that add up to eight?

3. Kate writes the factors of 10 in the boxes below and then adds them together. What should Kate's final result be?

4. What are the common factors of 9 and 18?

5. A number less than 50 is divisible by both 2 and 7 and the product of its two digits is 16. What is the number?

6. Work out the highest common factor (HCF) of 15 and 20 by completing the table below.

Number	Factors	HCF
15		
20		

   HCF =

7. What is the third multiple of 7 subtracted from the fifth multiple of 11?

8. Eight of the first nine multiples of a number are shown in random positions on the squares below. What is the missing multiple in the centre square?

   36

   27

      63   72

   45

   81

9. Write down the smallest number that is a multiple of both 6 and 9.

10. Pens are sold in packs of six. The packs are loaded into boxes with 15 packs contained in each box. How many pens are there in seven full boxes?

11. A fairground ride lasts seven minutes with a five minute break between rides. If the first ride starts at 09:30, at what time (in 24-hour clock format) will the fifth ride finish?

12. What is the lowest common multiple (LCM) of 9 and 15?

13. Which two of the following numbers are factors of 28 and multiples of 2?

    7   56   14   22   1   84   4

14. Two factors of 20 and two multiples of five are shown in the incomplete table below. What are the three numbers missing in the grey shaded cell?

Factors of 20	2, 4
Multiples of 5	15, 25
Numbers that are both factors of 20 and multiples of 5	?

15. The number represented by P is a factor of 24 and a multiple of 3. P is also greater than 7 and less than 22. What is the value of P?

Factors and Multiples - Intermediate

1. Write down all the factors of 78 in pairs, so that their products equal 78.

   .... , ... , ... , ...

2. What is the sum of the composite numbers in the list of numbers below?

   97   415   323   571   117   2802

   ....

3. The single digit numbers of a bicycle combination lock are the first five common factors of 36 and 54 in ascending order. What is the lock code?

   ....

4. What is the highest common factor (HCF) of 28, 56 and 70?

   ....

5. Petra completes the factor tree below in order to find the prime factors of 30. Write down the prime factors Petra should obtain.

   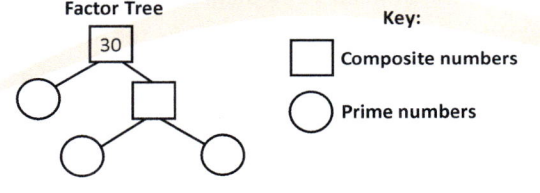

   ....

6. After carrying out the prime factorisation of a number N, the prime factors are revealed as 2, 2, 2 and 3. What is the number N?

   ....

7. The multiples below are the first eight multiples of a number. What is multiple A and the higher value multiple B?

   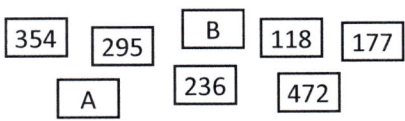

   A = ... , B = ...

8. What is the second smallest number that is a multiple of both 28 and 42?

   ....

9. If the third multiple of a number N is 15, what is the sum of the first five multiples of N?

   ....

10. A supermarket has a one-day special offer on eggs: *buy two boxes of six eggs and get one box of six eggs free.*
    (a) Which of the following possible quantities of special offer eggs could be the only quantity bought on the day?
    (b) Using answer (a), work out the total number of **boxes** of special offer eggs sold.

    3610   5396   4140   3910   4352   2445

    (a)............... , (b)...............

11. The lowest common multiple (LCM) of two numbers is 52. If the two numbers are both less than 20, what are the two numbers?

    ....

12. What is the lowest common multiple (LCM) of 12, 18 and 27?

    ....

13. Omar works out the seventh multiple of 18 and the highest common factor (HCF) of 28 and 42. Omar then writes down the lowest common multiple (LCM) of the two results. What should Omar's final answer be?

    ....

14. Sean wants to complete the Venn diagram below by entering factors of 26 and 39 in the three compartments of the diagram.
    (a) What factors should Sean enter in the central shaded area?
    (b) What is the lowest common multiple (LCM) of the three highest factors to be entered in the diagram?

    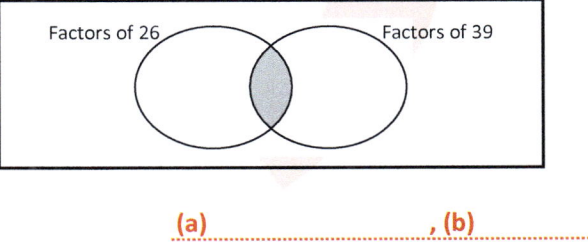

    (a)............... , (b)...............

15. I am a three-digit number with digits that add up to four. I am also the lowest common multiple (LCM) of both 20 and 44.
    (a) What number am I?
    (b) How many factors do I have?

    (a)............... , (b)...............

Factors and Multiples - Advanced

1. (a) What are the common factors of 48, 60 and 84?
   (b) What are the common factors found in 1(a) that are also prime numbers?

   (a) .... , (b) ....

2. Complete the factor tree below and use it to express 84 as a product of its prime factors.

   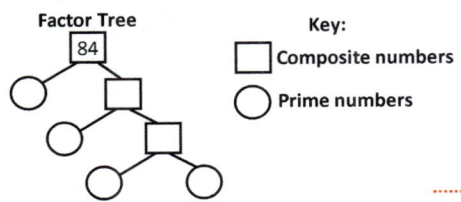

   ....

3. I am a two-digit composite number less than 40 with three different factors that add up to 31. In ascending order, my factors form a sequence with each term being five times the previous term. What number am I?

   ....

4. Complete the table of factors for areas A to G on the Venn diagram below.

   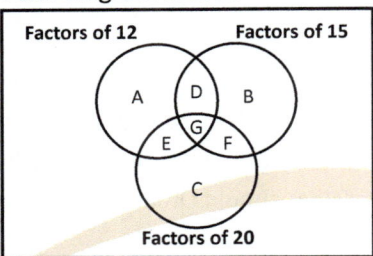

Area	Factors
A	
B	
C	
D	
E	
F	
G	

5. What are the prime factors of 910?

   ....

6. What is the product of the two highest common factors (HCFs) missing in the table below?

Number Pairs	HCF
54 and 72	
76 and 95	
Product	?

   ....

7. The sixth multiple of a number N lies halfway between 364 and 728. What is the value of N?

   ....

8. John, Saud and Sam play squash. John plays every six days, Saud plays every eight days and Sam plays every 12 days. If they all played squash today,
   (a) in how many days' time will John and Sam next play squash on the same day?
   (b) in how many days' time will they all next play squash on the same day?

   (a) .... days, (b) .... days

9. The ninth multiple of 86 is the sixth multiple of which number?

   ....

10. The number of people listening to an open-air pop concert at 2.00pm is equivalent to the ninth multiple of 76. At 4pm, the crowd number falls to the eighth multiple of 57. Express the crowd number at 4.00pm as a fraction (in its lowest terms) of the crowd number at 2.00pm.

    ....

11. Some of the consecutive multiples of a number have been entered in the table below. Work out the multiples that should be entered in cells A and B.

A			212
	159	212	
	212	265	B
212			

    A = ... , B = ...

12. Adele works out the lowest common multiple (LCM) of 22, 33 and 99 and then finds the seventh multiple of the result. What should Adele's final answer be?

    ....

13. Look at the unfilled Venn diagram below.
    (a) What is the highest common factor (HCF) of the numbers missing in the shaded central area?
    (b) What are the prime factors of the HCF in the above part (a)?

    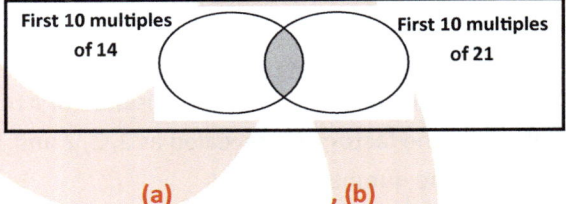

    (a) .... , (b) ....

14. The sixth multiple of a number N is equal to the sum of the prime factors of 39 multiplied by three. What is the value of N?

    ....

15. Work your way down the table below giving answers (a) to (d) in order.

The highest common factor (HCF) of 32, 40 and 56	?
The 91st multiple of answer (a)	?
The three different prime factors of answer (b)	?
The lowest common multiple (LCM) of answer (c)	?

    (a) .... (b) ....
    (c) .... (d) ....

Fractions and Decimals

Fractions and Decimals - Beginner

1. What is three-quarters of one hundred and sixty?

2. Write down the equivalent fractions represented by the shaded areas on the diagrams below.

   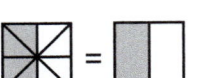

3. Write down the number of times the letter 'A' occurs in the word MATHEMATICAL as a fraction of all the letters in the word. Express your answer in its lowest terms.

4. Express the shaded 30° segment of cake shown below as a fraction of the whole cake.

   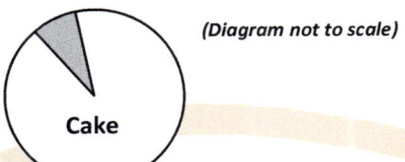
   (Diagram not to scale)

5. Subtract one-third from one-half.

6. Work out $^1/_2 \div 4$.

7. A wooden post is 3.4 metres (m) long. A length of 1.5m is cut off one end. What length of wood is left?

   .... m

8. The price of a T-shirt is £7.46. What is this cost to the nearest pound(£)?

   £ ....

9. What is the product of 0.3 and 0.02?

10. Kim uses 35.7% of the flour in a full packet to make some cakes. Express this percentage as a decimal.

11. A water tank contains 7.672 litres of water. Round this quantity to the nearest 100ml and express your final answer in litres (L).

    L

12. What is the common number missing in the two boxes below?

    $3.2 + 3.2 + 3.2 + 3.2 + 3.2 = \boxed{?}$, therefore, $\boxed{?} \div 3.2 = 5$

13. Express 5.42 as a mixed number in its simplest form.

14. Calculate the sum of the two fractional shaded areas on the diagrams below and convert the final fraction answer into a decimal.

    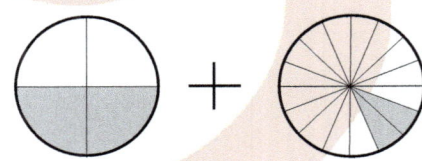

15. Work out the division below expressing your answer as an improper fraction in its lowest terms.

    $3.6 \div 0.25$

Fractions and Decimals - Intermediate

1. Write the fractions below in ascending order of size.

    $\frac{3}{8}$ $\frac{1}{6}$ $\frac{3}{5}$ $\frac{7}{8}$ $\frac{1}{4}$ $\frac{5}{6}$ $\frac{1}{3}$

    ....

2. Petra has made nine cakes to sell by the slice at the school fête. She cuts each cake into six slices and sells $6\frac{2}{3}$ cakes at the fête. How many cake slices are left unsold?

    ....

3. Find the fraction that lies halfway between $\frac{2}{3}$ and $\frac{4}{9}$.

    ....

4. Which two fractions equal $1\frac{3}{8}$ when added together?

    $\frac{5}{6}$ $\frac{3}{4}$ $\frac{1}{2}$ $\frac{1}{8}$ $\frac{7}{16}$ $\frac{5}{8}$

    ....

5. Work out the multiplication below, expressing your answer in mixed number format in its simplest form.

    $3\frac{5}{6} \times \frac{18}{8}$

    ....

6. Bilal printed out 96 sheets of text. $\frac{1}{12}$ of the sheets came out blotchy and $\frac{1}{16}$ came out with some missing text. How many sheets does Bilal need to reprint?

    ....

7. Round 74.352 litres to the nearest 100ml. Express your answer in ml.

    .... ml

8. Seven plane tickets cost £1,126. What is the cost of one plane ticket to two decimal places (2dp) of accuracy?

    £ ....

9. Work out the result of the number expression below.

    $\left(\dfrac{83.71 \times 25 \times 4 \times 1000}{2 \times 1000 \times 5}\right) \div 0.5$

    ....

10. Use the information on the diagram to work out the perimeter of the triangle with side lengths A, B and C.

    (Diagram not to scale)

    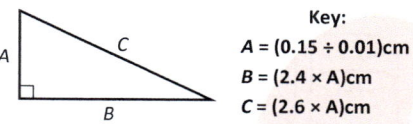

    Key:
    A = (0.15 ÷ 0.01)cm
    B = (2.4 × A)cm
    C = (2.6 × A)cm

    .... cm

11. Pari works out the missing common number *N* in the two number statements below, and then finds the value of *N* - 0.572. What should Pari's answer be?

    $N + N + N + N + N = 6.9$, therefore, $6.9 \div N = 5$

    ....

12. In a sale, Luke got 16% off a £430.50 television. He also bought a DVD player for 0.65 times the normal price of £98. How much did Luke pay altogether?

    £ ....

13. Write the mixed number below as a decimal to one decimal place (1dp).

    $11 \frac{5073}{10000}$

    ....

14. In a packet of party balloons, $\frac{3}{8}$ are coloured blue, $\frac{3}{16}$ are coloured yellow, and the remainder are coloured red.
    (a) Express as a decimal the number of red balloons in the packet.
    (b) If the number of balloons in the packet is 48, how many balloons are red?

    (a) .... , (b) ....

15. Write 10.64 as an improper fraction in its lowest terms.

    ....

Fractions and Decimals - Advanced

1. What is the missing proper fraction 'F' in the expression below? Express your answer in its simplest form.

   $1\,^5/_6 + F = 2\,^{17}/_{24}$

   ....

2. The diagram below shows three similar 2-litre capacity water tanks. Water from tanks 1 and 3 is poured into tank 2 until the quantity in all three tanks is the same. Working throughout in fractions, find the final quantity of water in each tank. Express your answer as an improper fraction in its simplest terms.

   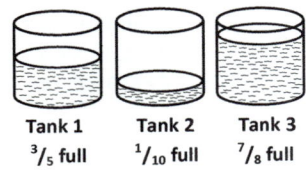

   Tank 1 $^3/_5$ full   Tank 2 $^1/_{10}$ full   Tank 3 $^7/_8$ full

   L

3. Fatou works out the result of $^2/_3 + 1\,^1/_6$, and also the result of $1\,^7/_8 - ^3/_{16}$. She then multiplies the two resulting fractions together. What is Fatou's final result expressed in mixed number format?

   ....

4. In the coin bags below, the number of 50p coins in bag 2 is N. The numbers of coins in bags 1, 3 and 4 are $^9/_5 \times N$, $^3/_8 \times N$ and $^3/_{10} \times N$ respectively. If N = half of 80, how much money in total is in all four bags? Express your answer in pounds (£).

   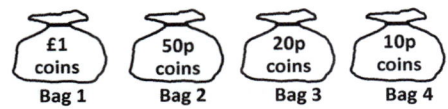

   £1 coins — Bag 1   50p coins — Bag 2   20p coins — Bag 3   10p coins — Bag 4

   £ ....

5. Look at the list of fractions below. Pierre divides the third largest fraction by the second smallest fraction and expresses his answer in mixed number format and in its lowest terms. What should Pierre's final answer be?

   $^{12}/_{18}$ $^{21}/_{24}$ $^{10}/_{16}$ $^{14}/_{20}$ $^9/_{12}$ $^5/_{10}$ $^{10}/_{25}$ $^{11}/_{33}$

   ....

6. Fabia has 48 sweets in a jar. She gives $^7/_8$ to Jane and Jane gives $^5/_6$ of her share to John. John then eats $^4/_7$ of his share. How many sweets has John got left?

   ....

7. Divide the number 98,675 by 12 and give your answer to three decimal places (3dp) of accuracy.

   ....

8. Hugo rounds the four numbers in the table according to the instructions given. What result should Hugo get for the sum of the four rounded answers?

Number	Number rounded to:	Rounded answer
6.82	the nearest whole number	
12.51	the nearest tenth	
8.739	the nearest hundredth	
0.2042	the nearest thousandth	
Sum		

   ....

9. What is the weight of 35 similar coins each weighing 0.0157kg? Express your answer to the nearest gram (g).

   .... g

10. A company makes bricks, each with a length (L) of 21.5cm, a width (W) of 10.25cm and a height (H) of 6.5cm. The length of each brick can vary by plus or minus 4mm, and the width by plus or minus 3mm. What would be the perimeter of the **top** of the **largest** sized brick expressed in cm?

    .... cm

11. Express the shaded area on the diagram as:
    (a) a mixed number in its simplest form.
    (b) an improper fraction in its simplest form.
    (c) a decimal correct to 3dp of accuracy.

    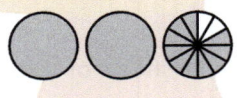

    (a)   (b)   (c)

12. If $7\,^3/_4 - 2\,^3/_8 = P$, what does $(^7/_8 \div ^3/_8) + P$ equal? Express your answer as a decimal to the nearest hundredth.

    ....

13. The diagram below gives dimension information for a small box of chocolate mints. What is the area of the smallest surface?

    (Diagram not to scale)

    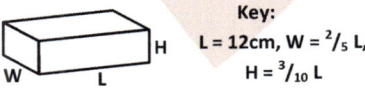

    Key: L = 12cm, W = $^2/_5$ L, H = $^3/_{10}$ L

    .... cm^2

14. What is the volume of the box in Q13 above?

    .... cm^3

15. If T = 4.25, what is $T^2 - T$? Give your answer correct to three decimal places (3dp) of accuracy.

    ....

Percentages, Ratios and Proportions

Percentages, Ratios and Proportions - Beginner

1. What is 5% of 80?

   ....

2. A DIY shop has 40 tins of paint for sale. In one day, they sell 10% of their stock. How many tins of paint are left unsold at the end of the same day?

   ....

3. Krishna has a mixture of blue, red and white counters in a bag. 23% are blue and 48% are red. Work out the percentage of white counters.

   .... %

4. Kim has saved £9 and her friend Mel has saved 50% more than Kim. How much money has Mel saved?

   £ ....

5. 40% of the stars below are to be shaded black. How many stars will be left unshaded?

   ....

6. Express the ratio 12:9 in its lowest terms.

   .... : ....

7. There are 80 visitors at a school fête, 32 of them being adults. What is the ratio of adults to children at the fête expressed in its simplest form?

   .... : ....

8. What is the missing number in the equivalent ratio shown below?

   14:? is equivalent to 2:3

   ....

9. The ratio of red to blue beads in a necklace is 5:4. If there are 20 blue beads, how many red beads are in the necklace?

   ....

10. The pattern of triangles shown below is repeated until the total number of triangles without a smiley face is 27. How many triangles in the completed pattern have a smiley face?

    ....

11. For the pattern of squares below, write as a fraction in its lowest terms, the proportion of squares that are shaded.

    ....

12. Nine of the 45 passengers on a coach are children. Express as a percentage the proportion of passengers that are children.

    .... %

13. The circles shown below are a repeating pattern. How many circles are there altogether if there are 30 shaded circles?

    ....

14. Two towns, 40km apart, are represented on a map with a scale of 1cm = 5km. How far apart are the towns on the map? Express your answer in cm.

    .... cm

15. A garden plan is drawn to a scale of 1:600. The garden is 5cm long in the drawing. What is the real length of the garden in metres (m)?

    .... m

Percentages, Ratios and Proportions - Intermediate

1. What is the missing percentage in the table below?

Fraction	Decimal	Percentage
3/50	0.06	?

   .... %

2. Three of the 75 apples in a box go bad. What percentage of apples are fit to eat?

   .... %

3. Twenty-five percent of the cement from a full bag remained after 12kg had been taken out. How many kilograms (kg) of cement was originally in the bag?

   .... kg

4. Forty-five percent of the 80 counters in a box have been removed. How many counters are left in the box?

   ....

5. Boxes of chocolates sold in a shop amounted to 0.2 of the total number at the start of day 1. Another 2/5 of the original total were sold on day 2. What percentage of boxes were left unsold at the end of day 2?

   .... %

6. Forty-one of the 50 passengers on a bus are adults. What percentage of passengers on the bus are children?

   .... %

7. In one year, an estate agent sells 72 flats and 48 houses. What is the ratio of flats to houses sold in its lowest terms?

   .... : ....

8. Some of the circles in the shape below are to be shaded. If the shaded to unshaded circle ratio will be 4:3, how many circles should be shaded?

   ....

9. In June, the ratio of dry days to wet days was 13:2. How many days in June were dry?

   .... days

10. In one hour, John observed red cars and blue cars pass by his house in the ratio of 2:7 and counted 108 in total. How many cars of each colour passed by?

    .... red cars, ... blue cars

11. What is the proportion of shaded hexagons in the pattern below?

    ....

12. In a café, out of all the drinks sold, the proportion of cold drinks was 35%. If the total number of drinks sold was 120, how many hot drinks were sold?

    ....

13. The square tiles below make up a pattern that is to be repeated along a bathroom wall. If there are to be 36 tiles with a cross, how many tiles will have a dot?

    ....

14. Using the information from the room plan shown below, which is drawn to a scale of 1cm = 0.5m, work out the area of the room in reality, in m^2.

    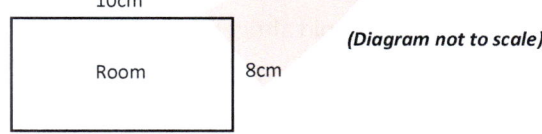

    (Diagram not to scale)

    .... m^2

15. The real distance between two roundabouts on a road is 400m. On a 1:10,000 scaled map, what is the distance in cm between the same two roundabouts?

    .... cm

Percentages, Ratios & Proportions - Advanced

1. Write 65.5%:
   (a) as a fraction in its simplest form.
   (b) in decimal format.

   (a) _____ , (b) _____

2. Cramley Gardens has 48,000 visitors a year. Thirty-two percent are adult males and 39.5% are adult females. Determine the numbers of adult males (M), adult females (F) and children (C) visiting the gardens.

   M = _____ , F = _____ , C = _____

3. The standard price of a car is £11,895. In a sale, Mr Patel bought the car for £1,675 less than the standard price. What percentage of the standard price did Mr Patel pay correct to two decimal places of accuracy?

   _____ %

4. In the number expression below, what is the value of N?

   N + (20% of 62.5) = (85% of 60) − 15

   _____

5. The population of a certain country is currently 1,185,760,000. The population increases by 1.5% each year. What will the population be one year from now?

   _____

6. Express the ratio 35:49:56:91 in its lowest terms.

   ___ : ___ : ___ : ___

7. Esme has 272 beads in a bag. 136 are yellow, 88 are green and the remainder are blue. What is the ratio of yellow to green to blue beads in its simplest form?

   ___ : ___ : ___

8. Tea, coffee, hot chocolate and bottled water are sold in a cafe in the ratio 15:11:7:4. If 75 teas are sold, how many drinks are sold altogether?

   _____

9. A baker sells quantities of thin, medium and thick sliced loaves of bread. Use the information in the table below to determine the ratio of thin to medium to thick loaves in its simplest form.

Bread Type	Number of loaves sold	
Thin sliced		= 25
Med. sliced	1.4 × 25	= ?
Thick sliced	80% more than 25	= ?

   ___ : ___ : ___

10. Kim, Omar, Nadia and Wayne share £25.60 in the ratio 1:2:5:8. Wayne then shares his received money between Tim and Pari in the ratio 2:3. How much money does Pari get?

    £ _____ .

11. Eighteen cars enter a car park every 6 minutes.
    (a) How many cars enter the car park in 5 minutes?
    (b) How many minutes does it take for 288 cars to enter the car park?

    (a) _____ , (b) _____ mins

12. A car travels 6 miles in 12 minutes. At a constant speed,
    (a) how long would it take for the car to travel 4 miles?
    (b) how many miles can the car travel in 7200 seconds?

    (a) _____ mins, (b) _____ miles

13. Some of the circles below are to be coloured red, some yellow and the remainder blue in order to create a single pattern. The proportion of yellow circles is to be $\frac{1}{3}$ and the ratio of yellow to red circles 4:3.
    (a) What will the proportion of blue circles be?
    (b) What will the ratio of yellow to blue circles be?

    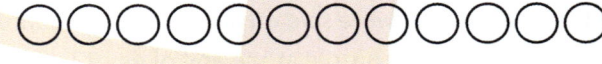

    (a) _____ , (b) ___ : ___

14. The width of the Atlantic Ocean at its widest is approximately 4,830km. What would be the ocean's width in millimetres (mm) on a map with a scale of 1cm = 300km?

    _____ mm

15. Two pictures P1 and P2 are to be mounted on a wall according to the scaled drawing details below. From the information given, determine:
    (a) the real length of L in metres.
    (b) the real combined area of both pictures P1 and P2.

    (Diagram not to scale)

    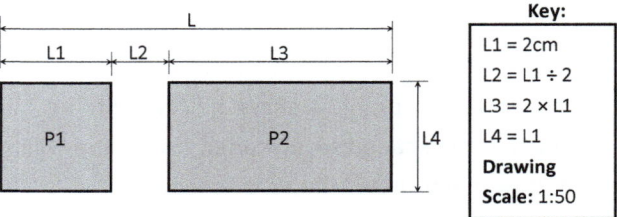

    Key:
    L1 = 2cm
    L2 = L1 ÷ 2
    L3 = 2 × L1
    L4 = L1
    Drawing Scale: 1:50

    (a) _____ m, (b) _____ m²

FIRST PAST THE POST

Algebra and Number Machines

Algebra and Number Machines - Beginner

1. If $x \div 2 = 1$, what is the value of x?

2. If $h - 5 = 11$, what is the value of h?

3. Expand the bracket $2(5x - 11)$.

4. If $y = 1$ and $z = 7$, solve $8(z - 2y)$.

5. A triangle is shown below. What is the expression for the area of the triangle?

   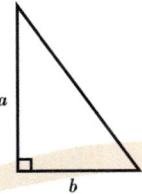

6. What number when cubed has an answer of 64?

7. Emma pays a monthly gym membership fee of x. What is the expression for the annual membership fee?

8. What is the value of $9x$ when $x = 1000$?

9. If $24 - 6c = 2c$, what is the value of c?

10. Using the equation $y = 6x + 23$, what is the value of A in the table?

x	-1	0	6
y	17	23	A

11. What is the output of the number machine below?

    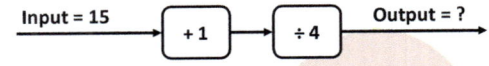

12. What is the output of the number machine below?

    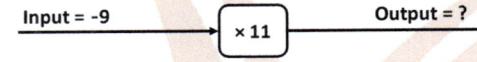

13. What is the input to the number machine below?

    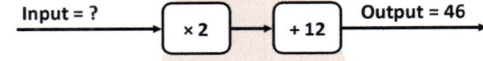

14. What is the output of the number machine below?

    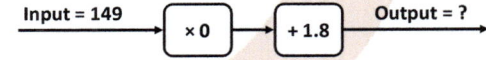

15. What is the output of the number machine below?

    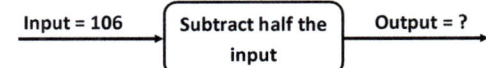

Algebra and Number Machines - Intermediate

1. Solve the equation $(x + 7) \div 8 = 2.5$.

2. Three years ago, a car was taken back to the garage where it had been built a quarter of a century earlier. How old is the car now?

3. The result of six times minus y added to sixty-four equals minus twenty. What is the value of y?

4. If $p = -0.75$ and $q = 4$, solve $2p(3q - 8p)$.

5. What is the simplified expression for the perimeter of the kite below?

   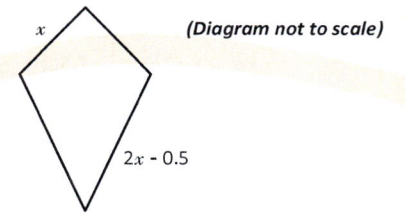
   (Diagram not to scale)

6. $22b - 11.2 = 108.8 - 8b$. What is the value of b?

7. Factorise $-56x^2 - 14x$

8. Form an expression for the perimeter of the triangle below and determine its value if $x = 18$cm and $y = 4$cm.

   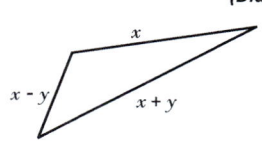
   (Diagram not to scale)

   .... cm

9. Some pentagons are shown below. Each unshaded pentagon was purchased for 55 pence while the price paid for each shaded pentagon is unknown. The total price paid for all the pentagons was £9.50. How much did one shaded pentagon cost in pence (p)?

   .... p

10. If $5w = 6(10 - 3x) - w$, what is the value of w when $x = 2$?

11. A function machine divides its input by 7 and subtracts 17 from the result to get the output. The input is 224. What is the output number?

12. What is the output of the number machine below?

    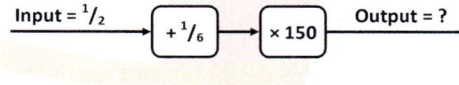

13. What is the input to the number machine below?

    Input = ? → ×5 → -45 → ÷8 → Output = 65

14. What is the output of the number machine below?

    Input = 5 → $+2^4$ → $\times\sqrt{225}$ → Output = ?

15. What is the output of the number machine below correct to one decimal place?

    Input 1 = 8.7
    Input 2 = 13.35
    → Input 2 - Input 1 → Output = ?

Algebra and Number Machines - Advanced

1. The perimeter of the symmetrical shape below is 657.6cm. What is the value of x?

   (Diagram not to scale)

   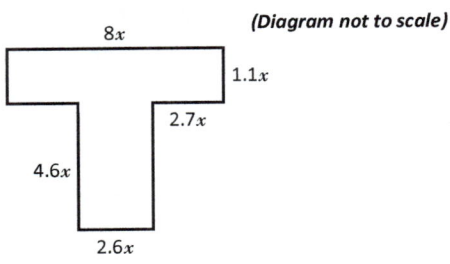

   .... cm

2. $z = 6(-a + 10b)(2b - c)$. What is the value of z if $a = -0.45$, $b = 0.95$ and $c = 0.5$?

   ....

3. What is the simplified expression for the output of the number machine below?

   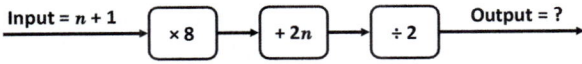

   ....

4. What is the value of x in the following equation?

   $56x + 143 = 42 + 109x - 5$

   ....

5. Claude had x pounds. He gave 15% of this to his son, one quarter to his daughter and spent the rest on music equipment. His daughter received £275.50. How much more money did he spend on music equipment compared to the amount he gave his son?

   £

6. What number is represented by the question mark in the number machine below?

   Input = 215 → $+6^3$ → × ? → − 25 → Output = 1052.5

   ....

7. What is the value of P in the following expression?

   $(24 \times 34) - (2095 \div 5) = 100P$

   ....

8. What number should replace the question mark in the expression below?

   $2780 + 2780 + 2780 + 1390 = ? \times 20$

   ....

9. What is the input to the number machine below?

   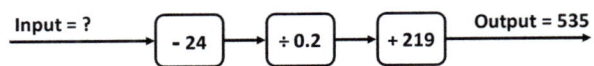

   ....

10. What is a simplified expression for the area of the shape below?

    (Diagram not to scale)

    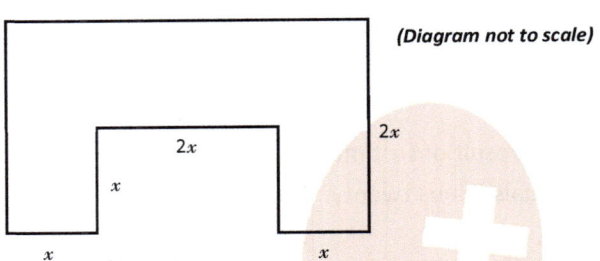

    ....

11. A negative number when cubed and then halved is -4,000. What is the number?

    ....

12. What is the output of the number machine below?

    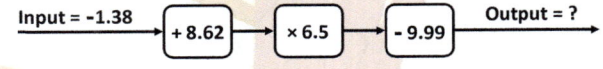

    ....

13. What is a simplified expression for the perimeter of the shape below?

    (Diagram not to scale)

    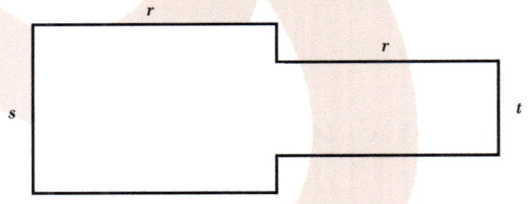

    ....

14. What is the value of y in the equation, $3y/5 - 2\frac{1}{3} = \frac{1}{2}$? Express your answer as an improper fraction.

    ....

15. What is the output of the Roman numeral number machine below? Give the output in Roman numerals.

    Input = CXXV → + L → ÷ V → − III → Output = ?

    ....

Averages and Representing Data

Averages and Representing Data - Beginner

1. The smallest number in a dataset is 4. The range of the dataset is 8. What is the largest number in the dataset?

    ....

2. What is the mean of the numbers below?

    0   1   2   3   4   5   6

    ....

Hasu has the following counters on her table. Using this information, answer questions 3 to 6.

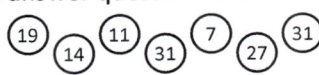

3. What is the mean? ....
4. What is the median? ....
5. What is the mode? ....
6. What is the range? ....

7. A set of people were asked what their shoe size was. The results are shown in the table below. What was the modal shoe size?

Shoe size	8	9	10	11	12
Frequency	2	5	4	3	1

    ....

8. Five temperatures are shown below. What is the average temperature?

Day	Temp (°C)
Monday	6
Tuesday	5
Wednesday	3
Thursday	9
Friday	7

    .... °C

9. One hundred and thirty trees were selected at random and their type determined. The results are shown in the pie chart. How many of the trees were Birch trees?

    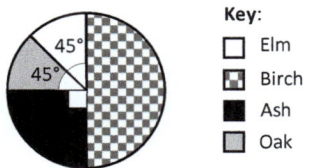

    ....

10. What is the average speed in miles per hour (mph)?

    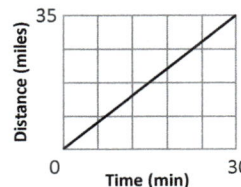

    .... mph

11. The chart below shows the number of pens given away by a bank. How many pens in total were given away?

    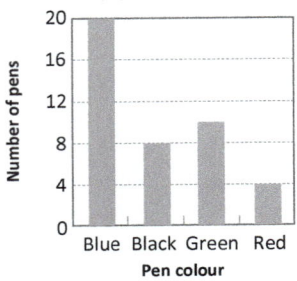

    ....

12. The table below shows the number of houses available in an area. How many houses have a garden?

No. of houses available	No. of bedrooms	Garage	Garden
2	1	No	No
9	2	No	Yes
7	2	Yes	No
5	3	Yes	Yes
2	4	Yes	Yes

    ....

13. Some pupils were asked if they liked swimming (S) or athletics (A). The results are shown in the Venn diagram below. What percentage of pupils liked both sports?

    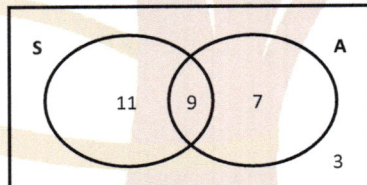

    .... %

14. The chart below shows the number of computers sold over the last seven weeks. On how many of the weeks were ≤900 computers sold?

    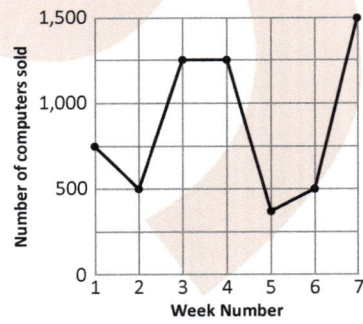

    ....

15. This tally table shows the number of phones owned by various people. How many people owned at least one phone?

Number of phones	Tally	Frequency
0	ꟿ︎ II	7
1	ꟿ︎ IIII	?
2	ꟿ︎ I	6
3	III	3

    ....

Averages and Representing Data - Intermediate

1. Expressed as an improper fraction, what is the average of the five fractions below?

   $\frac{4}{3}$ $\frac{2}{3}$ $\frac{5}{3}$ $\frac{3}{2}$ $\frac{8}{9}$

2. The weights of 6 pens are as follows. What is the median weight?

   6.5g 6.9g 5.4g 5.0g 6.3g 5.8g

   .... g

The following lengths (L) of objects A to G were recorded in cm. Using this information, answer questions 3 to 6.

Object	A	B	C	D	E	F	G
L (cm)	1.7	3.5	1.7	7.7	1.7	4.0	3.5

3. What is the mean? .... cm
4. What is the median? .... mm
5. What is the mode? .... cm
6. What is the range? .... mm

7. The table below shows the number of games won, drawn and lost by a team over 5 seasons. 3 points are awarded for a win, 1 point for a draw and 0 points for a loss. What is the percentage of seasons in which the team exceeded 35 points?

Season	Won	Drawn	Lost
1	10	4	4
2	9	3	6
3	11	2	5
4	10	6	2
5	8	7	3

.... %

8. One hundred and sixty eight children were asked what their favourite subject was. The results are shown in the pie chart below. How many children said music was their favourite subject?

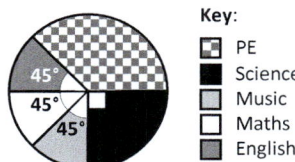

9. A number of adults were asked if they had a 50p coin, a £1 coin or a £2 coin on them. The results are shown in the Venn diagram below. How many had a 50p coin, a £2 coin or both?

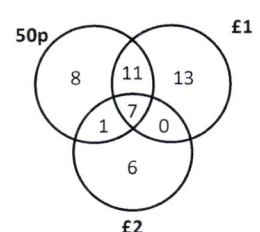

....

The chart below shows the temperature over a 7 day period. Using this information, answer questions 10 to 12.

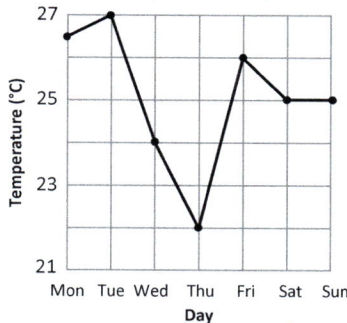

10. What is the average of the median daily temperature and the modal daily temperature? .... °C

11. What is the difference between the temperature on Friday and -11°C? .... °C

12. What is the mean daily temperature between Monday and Friday? .... °C

13. The chart shows distances covered by trains F and S. At the point where both trains meet, what is the difference between the average speed of each train?

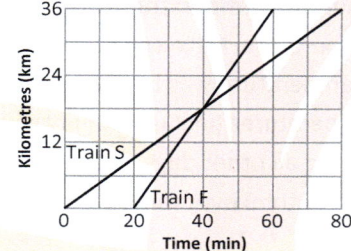

.... km/h

14. The chart shows science and history test results for 5 pupils. By how much was the mean test score in history higher than the mean test score in science?

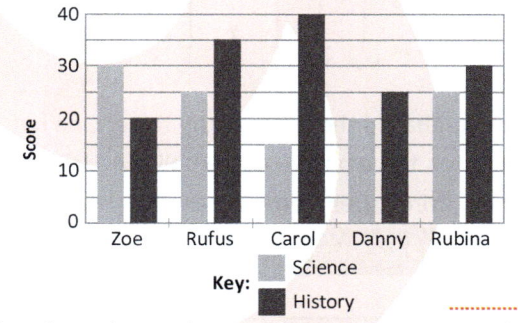

....

15. This chart shows the approximate conversion between litres and pints. Estimate how many pints 15 litres equal.

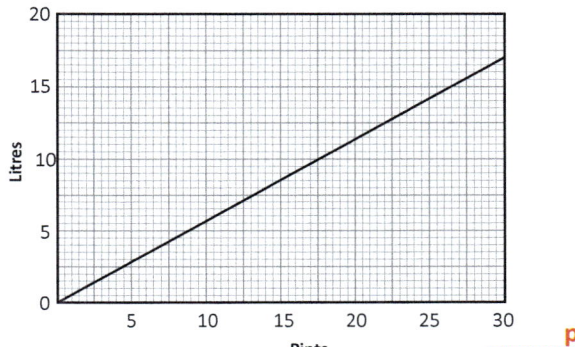

.... pints

Averages and Representing Data - Advanced

1. A dataset consists of 5 numbers. The mode of the dataset is 18, which occurs 3 times. The smallest number is $3/4$ of the mode and the largest number is 1.65 times the median value. What is the range of the dataset?

   ....

2. A number of people were asked if they had red, green and blue carpets in their homes. The results are shown in the Venn diagram. Fifty-two people had both red and green carpets in their homes. What fraction of people had both green and blue carpets, but not red carpets?

   Venn diagram: R region 78, R∩G 40, G region 89, R∩B 32, ? centre, G∩B 26, B region 73.
   Key: R = Red, G = Green, B = Blue

   ....

3. Mike went on holiday and the maximum daily temperatures during his break are shown on the chart. On days when the temperature was more than the median temperature, Mike spent £150, while on days when the temperature was between the mean and median temperatures (inclusive of both values), he spent £100. On all other days he spent £50. How much did he spend in total over the 6 days?

   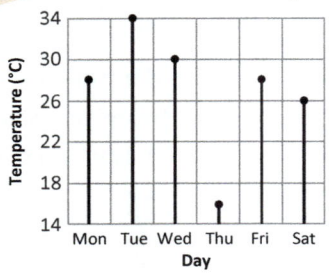

   £ ....

4. Prima purchased the items in the table. One hat costs three times the amount of one balloon. How much in total did Prima spend on the items?

Party item	Price per item	No. required	Total price
Hats	?	8	£2.40
Balloons	?	12	?
Plates	£0.15	20	?
		Total	?

   £ ....

5. The sum of four numbers is 88. The smallest number is 9 and the range is 26. The modal value (which is > the smallest value and < the largest value), occurs twice. What is the modal value?

   ....

6. Four values in a dataset add up to 14.96. The ratio of the values is 1:2:2:3. What is the range?

   ....

7. The number of cricket balls used in a town over a number of years is shown in the pictogram below. What was the mean number of balls used per year?

   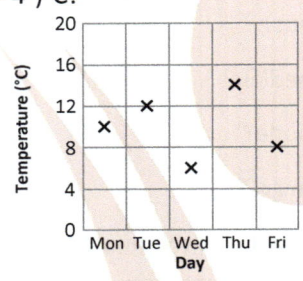

   ....

8. The chart below shows the temperatures over five days. On what day was the temperature 5°C above $(3^4 - \sqrt{144} - 4^3)$°C?

   Chart: Mon 10, Tue 12, Wed 6, Thu 14, Fri 8.

   ....

Using the table below, answer questions 9 to 13.

	Score					
Boys	3	4	1	8	5	3
Girls	10	9	2	7	1	1

9. What is the mean score for the girls?

   ....

10. What is the median score?

    ....

11. What is the average score?

    ....

12. What is the range minus the mode?

    ....

13. What fraction of students scored < 5?

    ....

14. A set of six values are shown below in Roman numerals. What is the result of multiplying the median and the mean of the dataset together. Give your answer in Roman numerals.

    XX   XXV   XVIII   XLVI   XXXII   LIX

    ....

15. The table below shows the numbers of coins in some bags. All the coins are identical in value. In total, £2.25 is in the bags. What is each coin worth in pence (p)?

Number of bags	Number of coins per bag
1	6
3	5
2	2
5	4

    p ....

Measures and Reading Scales

Measures and Reading Scales - Beginner

1. A wooden stick is 110 millimetres in length. What is its length, in centimetres?

   .... cm

2. What is the weight of the object below, in grams?

   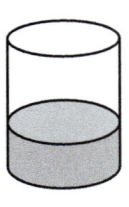

   .... g

3. How many millilitres of liquid are in the beaker below?

   0.8 litres

   .... ml

4. The weights of three objects (A, B and C) are shown in the table. What is the combined weight of all three objects, in grams?

Object	A	B	C
Weight	34kg	35kg	31kg

   .... g

5. If 1 mile = 1,760 yards, how many miles is 8,800 yards?

   .... miles

6. A container contains 11 pints of water. Approximately how many litres is this?
   Hint: 1 pint ≈ 0.5 litres.

   L

7. What reading is shown on the petrol gauge below, in litres? The reading is exactly halfway between the nearest two marks.

   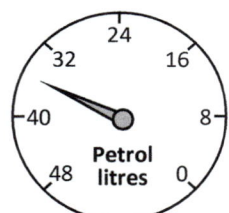

   L

8. An object is weighed on the scales below. How much does it weigh, in kilograms?

   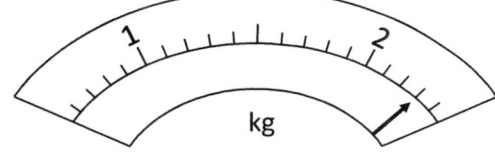

   .... kg

9. What temperature is shown on the thermometer?

   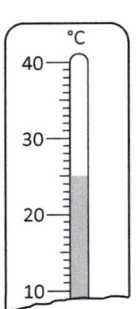

   .... °C

10. What reading is represented by the arrow on the ruler below, in millimetres? The reading is exactly halfway between the nearest two marks.

    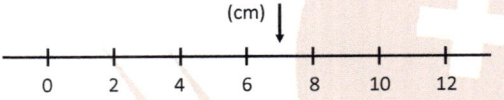

    .... mm

11. A diagram of a house is drawn at a scale of 1cm to 2.25m. The house is 9m high. How high is the house on the diagram?

    .... cm

12. How many kilograms short of 3 tonnes is the weight shown on the scale below?

    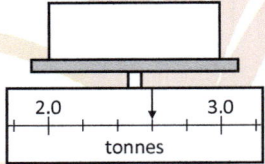

    .... kg

13. What is the difference between the two measurements R2 and R1 represented by the arrows on the ruler below?

    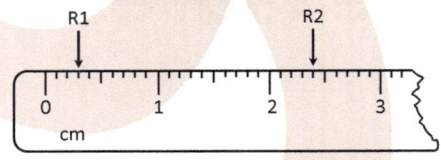

    .... cm

14. How many full 150ml glasses of water would it take to fill the container below to the level it is at currently, if it were empty?

    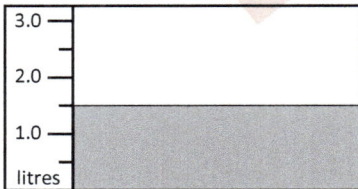

    ....

15. A map is produced at a scale of 1:50,000. What distance in kilometres would be represented by 2cm on the map?

    .... km

Measures and Reading Scales - Intermediate

1. What is the difference between 150,000 milligrams and 0.0025 tonnes in grams?

   .... g

2. The diagram below shows a remote control, which is 4.95cm in width. The numbers on the diagram represent the widths of buttons or blank sections on the control in millimetres. What is the width of the ON/OFF button?

   (Diagram not to scale)

   .... mm

3. If 1 gallon ≈ 4 litres, how many gallons is 55,000 millilitres?

   .... gallons

4. Carol's height is 80% of Pierre's height. What is Carol's height in centimetres?

   (Diagram not to scale)

   .... cm

5. Three identical printers weigh a total of 18.75 pounds. How much does each printer weigh in ounces? Hint: 1 pound = 16 ounces.

   .... ounces

6. Helen has 226.8 dollars in her bag. If £1 = $1.4, how many pounds has Helen got?

   £ ....

7. All the water in the jug below is added to a container which already has 650 millilitres of water in it. How much water will there be in the container?

   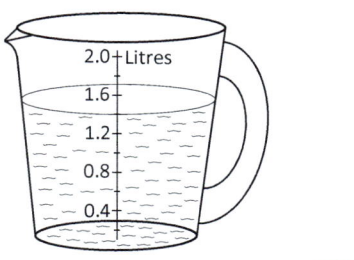

   .... ml

8. What is the average of minus 20°C and the temperature on the scale below? The reading is exactly halfway between the nearest two marks.

   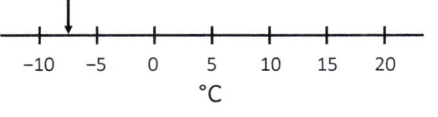

   .... °C

9. Surinder placed some butter on the scale at her local shop. How much did the butter cost if the price was 80p per 250 grams?

   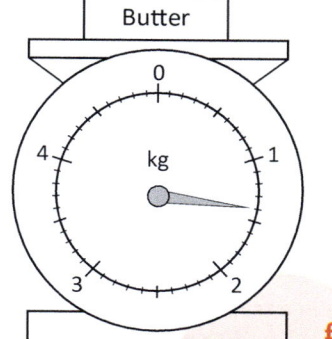

   £ ....

10. A map is produced at a scale of 1:3500. What distance on the map in centimetres would represent 280m in reality?

    .... cm

11. A rectangle is shown below along with a ruler. The width of the rectangle is 3 times its height. What is the area of the rectangle in square millimetres?

    (Diagram not to scale)

    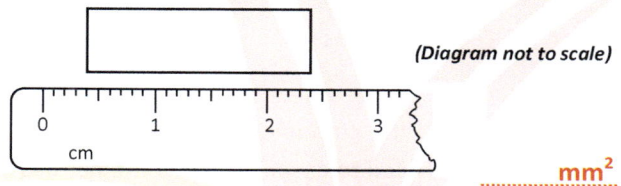

    .... mm^2

12. Five identical boxes and a rice container are shown on the scales below. Each box weighs 280 grams. How much does the rice container weigh in grams?

    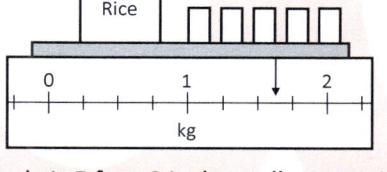

    .... g

13. Cindy is 5 foot 9 inches tall. Approximately, how far off 2 metres tall is she? Hint: 1 foot = 12 inches and 1 inch ≈ 2.5 centimetres.

    .... m

14. What is the difference between the lengths of nails A and B in metres to two decimal places?

    (Diagram not to scale)

    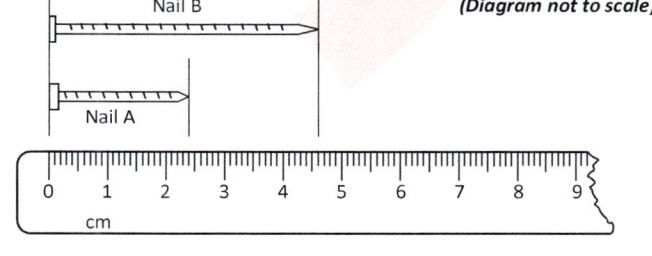

    .... m

15. Riz creates a scaled drawing of a wall. The scale is 1:220. If the full length of the wall in the drawing is 2.8cm, what is the length of the wall in reality?

    .... m

Chapter 8: Measures and Reading Scales - Advanced

1. Using the fact that 1 pint ≈ 500 millilitres, approximately (to 1dp), how many quarter pint glasses of water would need to be added to the water in the tank below to fill it to its 2.7-litre capacity?

   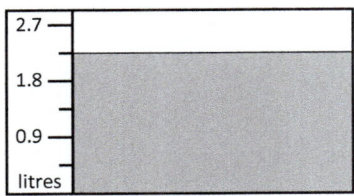

   ....

2. The line graph below shows the distance travelled over time during a train journey. Between the times of 1,800 seconds and 3600 seconds into its journey, what was the average speed of the train in yards per hour? Hint: 1 mile = 1760 yards.

   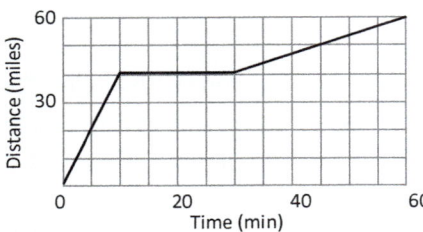

   .... yards/h

3. Bev has a three-litre container of water that is three-quarters filled to capacity. The container has a leak where 40 millilitres of water are lost every 30 seconds. How many litres of water will be left in the container after 17.5 minutes?

   L

4. Mohit draws a scaled drawing of a square. The scale is 1:55,000. What is the area of the square in m² if the length of one side of the square in the drawing is √256 millimetres?

   .... m²

5. How much weight (in kilograms) would need to be removed from the right-hand side of the scales below to achieve balance?

   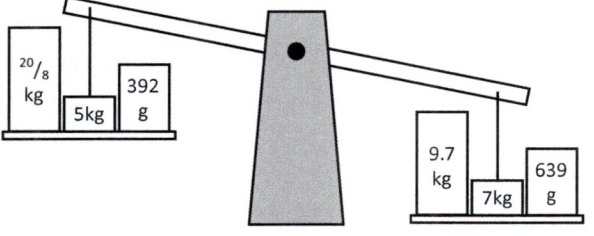

   .... kg

6. Alessandro threw a shot put a distance of 18.65 metres. Approximately how many inches did he throw the shot put? Hint: 3 feet ≈ 1000 millimetres and 1 foot = 12 inches.

   .... inches

7. Approximately what is 0.817 tonnes in ounces if 1 ounce ≈ 25 grams?

   .... ounces

8. Eight identical plastic crates have a combined weight of 12 stone and 8 pounds. What is the combined weight of 22 identical plastic crates in ounces? Hint: 1 stone = 14 pounds and 1 pound = 16 ounces.

   .... ounces

9. A half-litre carton of milk costs 50 pence to purchase while a two-litre carton of milk costs £1.20 to purchase. Mrs Cooper bought 4 of the smaller cartons and 7 of the larger cartons. What was the average price she paid per litre of milk?

   £ ....

10. The diagram below shows four objects labelled A, B, C and D on a set of scales. Objects A, B and C all weigh the same amount, but object D is seven times the weight of object A. How much does object D weigh in tonnes?

    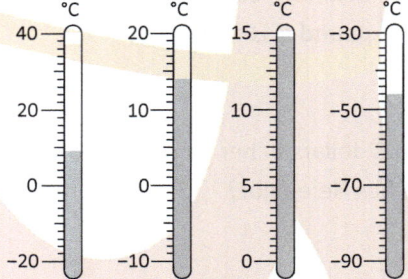

    .... tonnes

11. What is the outcome of adding 17.101cm, 4708mm and $2\,^5/_8$cm, and presenting the result in cm to two decimal places?

    .... cm

12. What is the median temperature shown on the thermometers below?

    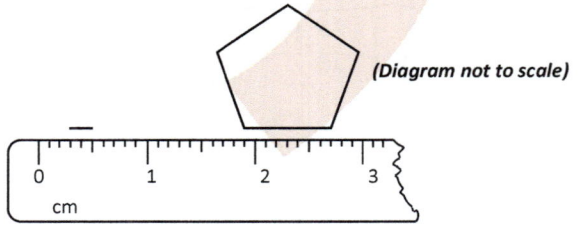

    .... °C

13. A straight line, a regular pentagon and a ruler are shown below. How many of the straight lines would be needed to build the pentagon? Give your answer in Roman numerals.

    (Diagram not to scale)

    ....

14. The diameter of a coin is 20mm. How many coins would fit across a length of $2\,^2/_5$m?

    ....

15. A toy cuboid block with length 5.5cm, width 2.5cm and height 3cm is a model of a real-life metal block at a scale of 1:20. What is the volume of the real-life block in cubic metres?

    .... m³

Dates, Times and Timetables

Dates, Time and Timetables - Beginner

1. How many days long is the month of January?

   .... days

2. If today is Monday 25th November, what day of the week was 10th November?

   ....

3. John buys some milk on the 18th of September. It expires on the 23rd of September. For how many days can he drink the milk before it expires?

   .... days

4. Use the incomplete calendar below to determine the date represented by the question mark.

   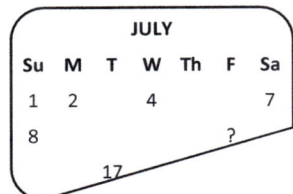

   ....

5. Cassie goes to the gym once a week on a Friday. If today is Monday the 1st of October, how many times will she visit the gym this month?

   ....

6. How many hours are between 10.00am and 4.00pm?

   .... hr

7. How many minutes are 480 seconds?

   .... min

8. The clock face below shows the time one afternoon. What is the time in 12-hour clock format?

   ....

9. The time now is 9.10pm. What will the time be in three-quarters of an hour in 12-hour clock format?

   ....

10. What is half past midnight in 24-hour clock format?

    ...... : ......

11. What is 7.19pm in 24-hour clock format?

    ...... : ......

12. A train leaves Hull station at 06:25 and calls at the following stations on its way to Grantham. How many minutes does the whole journey take?

Station	Arrival Time
Brough	06:37
Howden	06:49
Selby	07:00
Doncaster	07:21
Retford	07:41
Grantham	08:03

    .... min

13. The timetable for boats A, B and C to travel from Runnymede to Windsor are shown below. If all three boats complete their journey in the same time, what time will boat B arrive at Windsor? Express your answer in 24-hour clock format.

	Boat A	Boat B	Boat C
Runnymede	10:00	13:15	16:30
Bells of Ouzeley	10:25	13:40	16:55
Datchet	11:02	14:17	17:32
Windsor	11:30	?	18:00

    ...... : ......

14. The table below shows a timetable for a bus leaving Guildford at 6.40pm. The bus calls at the stops below on its way to Woking. Three-quarters of an hour after leaving Guildford, the bus has a flat tyre. What stop would the bus have called at next at this point?

Stop	Time
Stoughton	18:48
Worplesdon	18:54
Pirbright	18:58
Brookwood	19:01
Knaphill	19:10
Woking	19:28

    ....

15. Lauren walks past points A, B, C and D on her journey from home to work in the morning. She leaves home at 7.25am and arrives at work at 8.15am. She passes by point B after 50% of her journey is complete. At what time, in 12-hour clock format, does she pass point B?

    ....

Dates, Time and Timetables - Intermediate

1. How many days are there in total in April, May and June?

   .... days

2. If today is Monday 1st February in a non-leap year, what fraction of the days in this month will be weekdays?

   ....

3. Eric returned from his holiday on Monday 5th of October. He left for his holiday exactly 40 days earlier. On what day of the week did Eric leave for his holiday?

   ....

4. The table below shows the years of birth for 5 people in Roman numeral format. Who was born first?

Name	Year of birth
Mary	MMVI
Jai	MMXI
Yousef	MCM
Peter	MCML
June	MM

   ....

5. In any four-year calendar period, how many days are there in total?

   .... days

6. Clock A shows a time of 9.15pm and zero seconds. Clock B shows a time of 9.12pm and 30 seconds. Clock A loses 30 seconds every day, while clock B does not gain or lose any time. In how many days will both clocks show exactly the same time?

   .... days

7. What is the difference in minutes between 13:34 and 3.49pm on the same day?

   .... min

8. The table shows the time difference (in hours) of some cities relative to London. If the time is 11.25pm in Tokyo, what is the time in London in 24-hour clock format?

City	Time difference (hours) relative to London
Perth	+8
Baltimore	-5
Tokyo	+9
Karachi	+5
Los Angeles	-8
Athens	+2

   .... : ....

9. How many hours are there in 2 $\frac{2}{3}$ days?

   .... hr

10. What is the difference in minutes between the two times shown on the clocks below (both clocks show times from the same morning)?

    .... min

11. In a sixth of an hour it will be twenty past seven in the morning. What is the time now in 12-hour clock format?

    ....

12. Trains X and Y were scheduled to complete their journeys in the same time. However, train Y was delayed for an additional 720 seconds between Aberdeen and Dyce. What time, in 24-hour clock format, did train Y arrive at Dyce?

	Train X	Train Y
Dundee	10:34	20:07
Arbroath	10:51	20:24
Montrose	11:05	20:38
Stonehaven	11:26	20:59
Aberdeen	11:46	21:19
Dyce	12:08	?

    .... : ....

13. The table below shows a bus timetable from York to Colton. Sixty percent of the way through its journey, what stop had the bus called at last?

Stop	Time
York	15:31
Middlethorpe Grove	15:38
Bishopthorpe	15:45
Appleton Roebuck	15:54
Bolton Percy	15:58
Colton	16:07

    ....

14. What is the range of journey times (in minutes) of the three buses in the table below to complete their routes from the library to the museum?

	Bus A	Bus B	Bus C
Library	09:30	09:45	10:00
High Street	09:43	10:01	10:19
Station	09:55	10:19	10:34
Museum	10:23	10:38	10:58

    .... min

15. Jan's train left Gateshead 5 minutes early, at 09:16. It arrived in Peterborough 6 minutes late, at 11:53. How many minutes would the journey have taken if the train had left and arrived on time?

    .... min

Dates, Time and Timetables - Advanced

1. Expressed as a mixed number, what is the average number of days per month for all months between January and September, inclusive of both months? Assume it is not a leap year. .... days

2. How many minutes later is 22:19 on Tuesday than 00:07 the previous Sunday? .... mins

3. Circle the time in the table below that is closest to the morning time shown on the Roman numeral clock face.

Times
10.02am
13:20
90 minutes before noon
3.75 hours after 8.00am
700 seconds before 11.15am

4. Ania's day at school starts at 8.35am and consists of the following sessions. At what time, in 12-hour clock format, does school finish?

Session	Duration
Registration	20 minutes
Lesson 1	1.1 hours
Lesson 2	1.1 hours
Break	900 seconds
Lesson 3	1.2 hours
Lesson 4	1.2 hours
Lunch	40 minutes
Lesson 5	1.15 hours

....

5. Tommy started a short course on Tuesday 15th January. He completed the course on the 4th March. On which day of the week did Tommy complete the course? Assume it is a leap year. ....

6. The table below shows the times at which 5 trains called at stations between London and Brussels. Trains 2, 3, 4 and 5 did not call at all the stations. What was the median time, in minutes, for a train to complete its journey?

	Train 1	Train 2	Train 3	Train 4	Train 5
London	07:20	08:30	09:27	12:04	13:57
Ebbsfleet	07:37	---	09:45	---	14:15
Ashford	07:57	---	---	---	---
Calais	09:29	---	---	---	---
Lille	10:07	---	11:54	14:26	16:24
Brussels	10:42	11:28	12:33	15:05	17:03

.... mins

7. How many seconds less than 280.5 minutes is the number of minutes in 4 3/5 hours? .... sec

8. Each week, Danica teaches nine Year 5 classes and six Year 4 classes. Each Year 5 class lasts 55 minutes and each Year 4 class lasts 45 minutes. If she teaches 51 hours a week, what percentage of this does she spend teaching Year 4 and Year 5 classes? .... %

9. Jess spent 50% of the days in a leap year studying and 60% of the days the following year studying. How many days in total was she studying over the two years? .... days

10. This clock shows the time one morning. Use the clock and number machine below to work out the output time in 12-hour clock format.

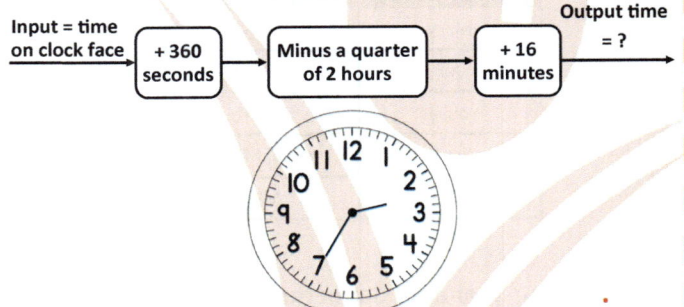

....

11. How many full weeks is equivalent to 60,480 minutes? .... weeks

12. Amit catches the same train (see timetable below) every morning from Westminster to Barking for 270 days in a year. How many hours does he spend making this journey during the year?

Station	Time
Gloucester Road	14:50
Westminster	15:02
West Ham	15:26
Barking	15:38

.... hr

13. What percentage of months containing less than 31 days have more than 8 characters in their name? .... %

14. If a week starts on Sunday 3rd at 00:00, what date and time (12-hour clock format) is exactly three-quarters of the way through the week? ....

15. Jo lives at West Shore and took the 11:20 bus to Conwy, which arrived at 11:45. Amy caught the 10:15 bus from Llandudno to Conwy, which arrived at 10.45. Brian caught the 10:57 bus from the Promenade to Conwy, which arrived at 11:15. What was the average journey time for the three people, in seconds? .... sec

Lines, Angles and Bearings

Lines, Angles and Bearings - Beginner

1. Circle the horizontal line from the lines below.

   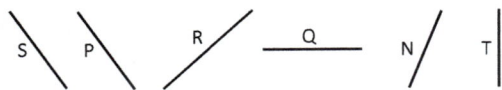

2. What is the length of the line that is parallel to line D below?

   (Diagram not to scale)

   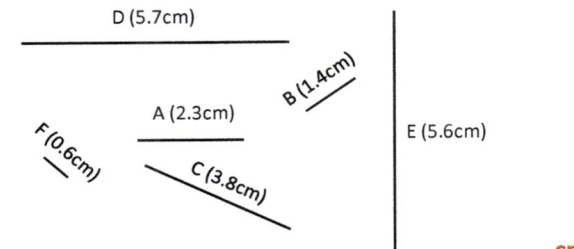

   .... cm

3. Can an oblique line ever be parallel to the *x*-axis?

   ....

4. What is the sum of the interior angles of a quadrilateral?

   ....°

5. What is the size of angle $k°$?

   (Diagram not to scale)

   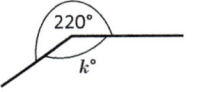

   ....°

6. What is the name of an angle which is less than 90°?

   ....

7. What is the size of angle $j°$ in the isosceles triangle below?

   (Diagram not to scale)

   ....°

8. What is the size of angle $q°$ in the diagram below?

   (Diagram not to scale)

   ....°

9. What is the size of angle $p°$ in the diagram below?

   (Diagram not to scale)

   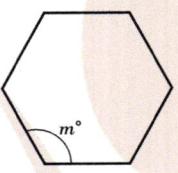

   ....°

10. Which of the angles below is obtuse in size?

    93°   90°   190°   45°   181°   478°

    ....°

11. What is the size of angle $m°$ in the regular polygon?

    ....°

12. What is the opposite direction to west?

    ....

13. On a compass, how many right angles are between north and south?

    ....

14. In which diagram (A to E) below, is the house located southwest of the train station?

    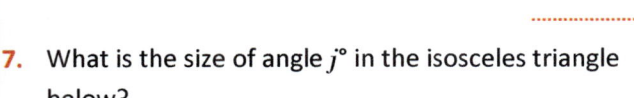
    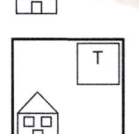
    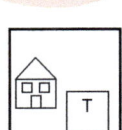

    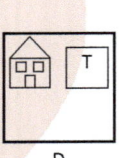
    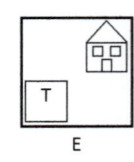

    A   B   C   D   E

    ....

15. Which labelled point on the shape below is directly east of point M?

    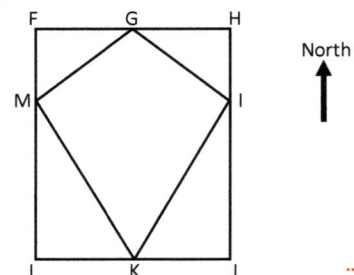

    ....

Lines, Angles and Bearings - Intermediate

1. The distance between two parallel lines is 1870 $^3/_5$ mm. What is the distance between the two lines in metres to two decimal places?

   .... m

2. What is the median length of the lines that are perpendicular to Line A below?

   (Diagram not to scale)

   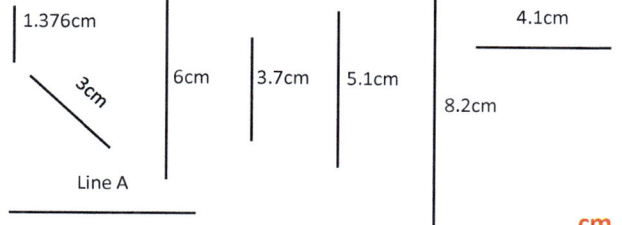

   .... cm

3. The length of the shorter diagonal of the kite below is 40% the length of the longer diagonal of the kite. What is the length of the shorter diagonal?

   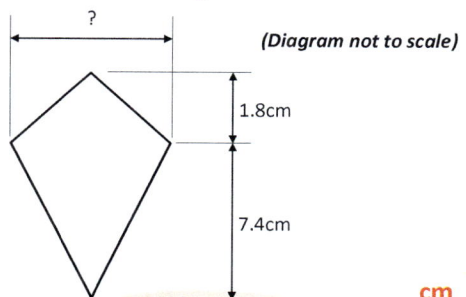

   (Diagram not to scale)

   .... cm

4. One interior angle in an irregular hexagon is 142.79°. What must the sum of the other interior angles be?

   .... °

5. What angle is $^5/_6$ of three right angles?

   .... °

6. Through what angle must the wheel be turned clockwise so that point P meets the horizontal arrow?

   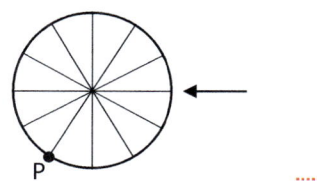

   .... °

7. What is the size of angle $x°$ in the symmetrical trapezium below?

   (Diagram not to scale)

   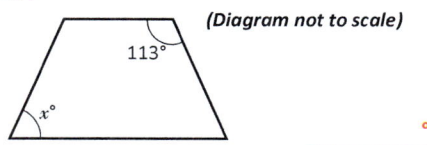

   .... °

8. An isosceles triangle is shown below. What is the size of angle $a°$?

   (Diagram not to scale)

   .... °

9. What is the average size of angles $t°$ and $u°$ below?

   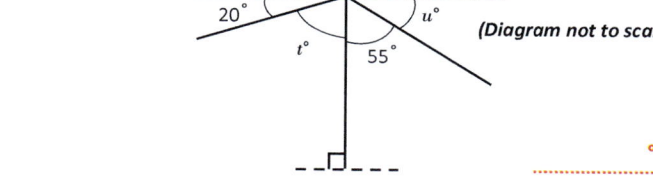

   (Diagram not to scale)

   .... °

10. If the hour hand on a clock face turns 150° anticlockwise from 3.00pm, what will the new time be?

    .... :

11. What is the size of angle $b°$ in the regular pentagon below?

    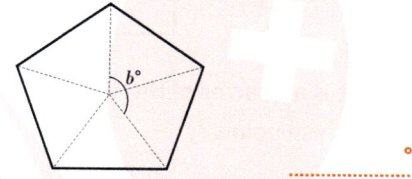

    .... °

12. On a compass, how many degrees clockwise is the turn from northeast to west?

    .... °

13. James is facing south and turns through 495° anticlockwise. In which direction is James now facing?

    ....

14. Bharti is standing on the grey shaded square in the grid below. She is facing north. In which direction from her is the square with the number equivalent to Roman numerals LI on the grid?

    N ↑

1	52	3	40	5
6	51	88	49	17
10	18		84	45
16	101	8	29	20
81	22	63	24	90

    ....

15. Below, if the post box is south of Sophie and the library is southeast of her, in what direction is the hospital from Sophie?

    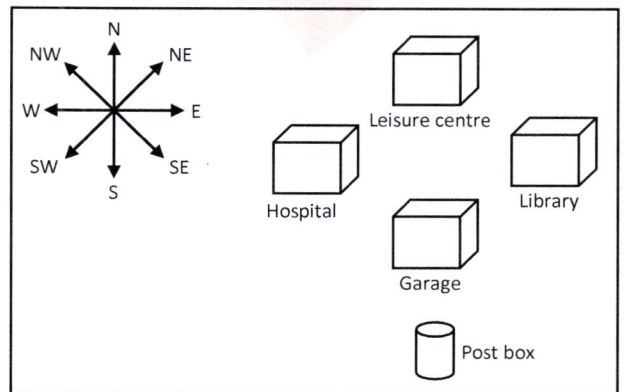

    ....

© 2017 ElevenPlusExams.co.uk   39   COPYING STRICTLY PROHIBITED

Lines, Angles and Bearings - Advanced

1. Two interior angles in a triangle are $37\frac{5}{8}°$ and $85\frac{3}{5}°$. What is the size of the last angle? Give your answer in decimal format.

   ....°

2. Nigel counts the number of sides that are perpendicular to side 1 below. He cubes the result and then subtracts 17.941 from the answer. What value should he obtain?

   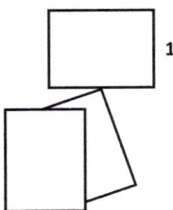

   ....

3. What is a quarter of the size of angle A shown on the clock face below?

   ....°

4. The angles in a quadrilateral are in the ratio 3:4:11:6. What is the size of the largest angle?

   ....°

5. A ball on a snooker table bounces off Cushion C before going into Pocket P. What is angle $n°$ if angles $m°$ and $n°$ are the same?

   (Diagram not to scale)

   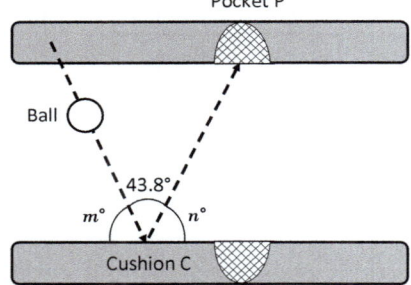

   ....°

6. What is the size of angle $k°$?

   (Diagram not to scale)

   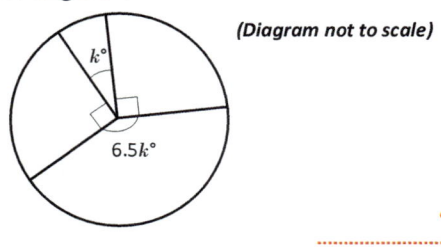

   ....°

7. What is the sum of the obtuse angles below?

   78°   101.19°   873.55°   170.04°   0.91°   289.46°   90.73°

   ....°

8. What is the difference in size between angles $s°$ and $t°$ below?

   (Diagram not to scale)

   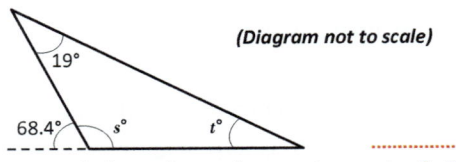

   ....°

9. The smallest angle in an irregular pentagon is $q°$. The next largest angle is twice the angle $q°$. The next largest angle is 2.5 times the value of $q°$ and the fourth largest angle is 3 times the value of $q°$. The last angle is 6.5 times the value of $q°$. What is the size of the largest angle?

   ....°

10. What is the size of angle $x°$ in the regular polygon below?

    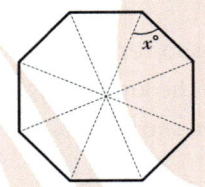

    ....°

11. Which of the instructions should be followed to travel on the shaded path from the START square to the FINISH square? (F = forward, L = turn left, R = turn right).

    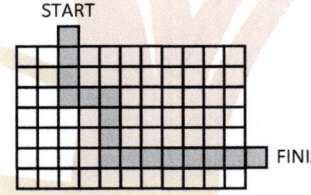

    a. F 3, L 90°, F 2, L 90°, F 3, L 90°, F7.
    b. F 3, L 90°, F 2, R 90°, F 3, L 90°, F7.
    c. F 3, R 90°, F 2, L 90°, F 3, L 90°, F7.
    d. F 2, L 90°, F 2, R 90°, F 4, L 90°, F7.
    e. F 3, R 90°, F 3, L 90°, F 3, L 90°, F7.

12. What is the size of angle $y°$?

    (Diagram not to scale)

    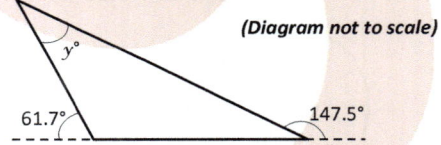

    ....°

13. In degrees (°), what is the size of 2.85 right angles?

    ....°

14. Each of the following 5 people are at one of the numbered points on the diagram below. Zoha is east of Jason and Kerstin is west of Ardan. Amit is south of Ardan. What direction is Amit from the school?

    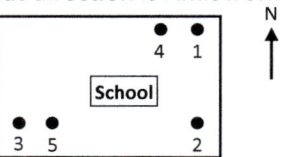

    ....

15. What is 3,972.5° divided by 20 to two decimal places?

    ....°

2D Shapes, Perimeter, Area and Symmetry

2D Shapes, Perimeters, Areas and Symmetry - Beginner

1. What is the name of the shape below?

   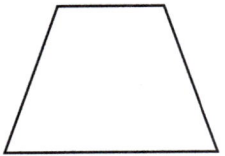

   ....

2. What is the name of a triangle in which all three sides are of different lengths?

   ....

3. How many pairs of parallel sides does a regular octagon have?

   ....

4. A parallelogram is shown below. What is the length of Y?

   (Diagram not to scale)

   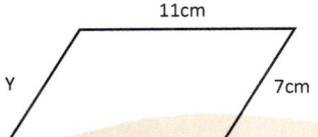

   .... cm

5. The radius of a circle is 16cm. What is its diameter?

   .... cm

6. A side of a kite is selected at random. How many of its remaining sides are the same length as that selected?

   ....

7. What is the name of a polygon with seven sides?

   ....

8. What is the area of the oblong below?

   (Diagram not to scale)

   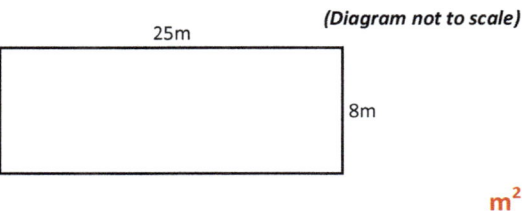

   .... m^2

9. A square has a perimeter of 44mm. What is the area of the square?

   .... mm^2

10. By how many cm is the perimeter of the rectangle larger than the perimeter of the triangle below?

    (Diagram not to scale)

    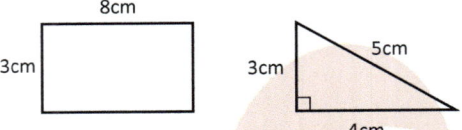

    .... cm

11. Two rectangles are shown below. If each square that makes up the rectangles has an area of $10mm^2$, what is the combined area of R1 and R2?

    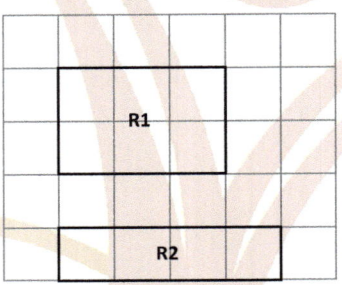

    .... mm^2

12. What is the area of the triangle below?

    (Diagram not to scale)

    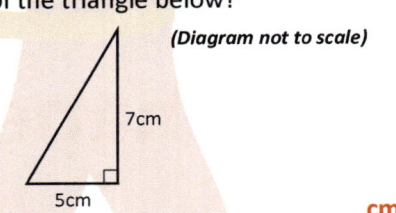

    .... cm^2

13. How many lines of symmetry does an equilateral triangle have?

    ....

14. What is the order of rotational symmetry of the rhombus below?

    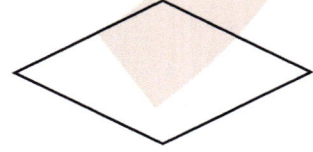

    ....

15. Which shape below (1 to 4) is shown with an incorrect line of symmetry?

    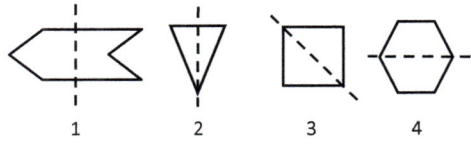

    ....

2D Shapes, Perimeters, Areas and Symmetry - Intermediate

1. What is the total number of sides of the shapes below?

2. A shape has three interior acute angles, two of which are equal in size. The shape also has one line of symmetry. What is the shape?

3. Which of the polygons below looks most like a circle?

   a. Nonagon
   b. Pentagon
   c. Decagon
   d. Heptagon
   e. Hexagon
   f. Octagon
   g. Triangle

4. What is the radius of one of the three identical circles below in centimetres?

   (Diagram not to scale)

   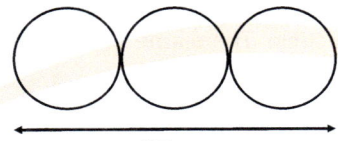

   330mm

   .... cm

5. What fraction of the shapes below are polygons with at least one pair of parallel sides?

    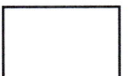 

6. How many sides of equal length do 46 identical, regular quadrilaterals have?

7. What is the name of the regular polygon whose interior angles sum to 1260°?

8. The combined length of four sides of a regular heptagon is 2156cm. What is the perimeter of the heptagon?

   .... cm

9. The area of the square below is 169cm². What is the area of the shaded triangle?

   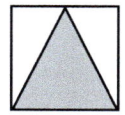

   .... cm²

10. What is the expression for the area of the rectangle below?

    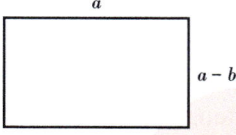

11. What is the perimeter of the shape below?

    (Diagram not to scale)

    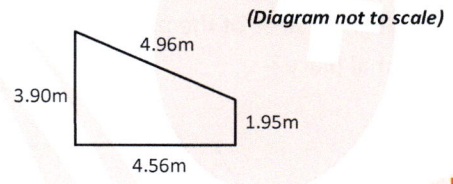

    .... m

12. A shape is shown on the grid below. If each square on the grid has an area of 9cm², what is the area of the shape?

    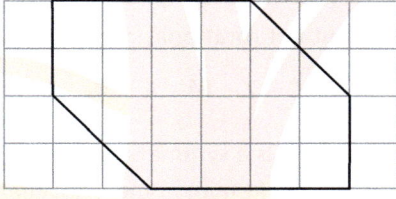

    .... cm²

13. How many of the following capital letters have at least one line of symmetry through their centre?

    P R N A L S C

14. Part of a regular shape is shown below along with two lines of symmetry. How many lines of symmetry will the full shape have?

    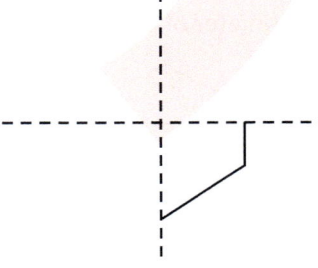

15. What is the average order of rotational symmetry of the five shapes below?

    2 equilateral triangles   1 square

    1 parallelogram   1 rectangle

2D Shapes, Perimeters, Areas and Symmetry - Advanced

1. The mean length of the sides of the shape below is 490cm. What is the length of the side labelled with the question mark?

   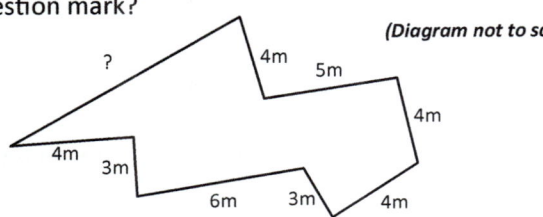
   (Diagram not to scale)

   .... m

2. The shortest side of a rectangle is $1.4x$. The longest side of the rectangle is $2.3x - 3.2$. What is a simplified expression for the perimeter of the rectangle?

   ....

3. What is the area of the parallelogram below, to one decimal place?

   (Diagram not to scale)
   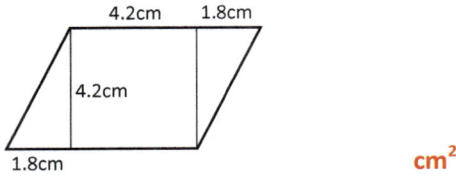

   .... cm^2

4. What percentage of the capital letters below have line symmetry but not rotational symmetry?

   S C Z M E W I J

   .... %

5. The shape below is a symmetrical letter T with its measurements in Roman numerals. What is its perimeter in Roman numerals?

   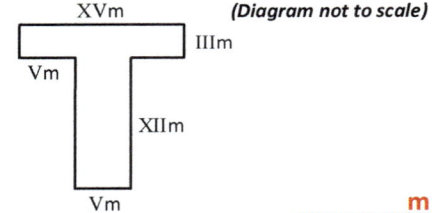
   (Diagram not to scale)

   .... m

6. A rhombus and 16 identical circles are shown below. The four corners of the rhombus are at the centre points of four circles. Each circle has a radius of 1.5cm. What is the perimeter of the rhombus?

   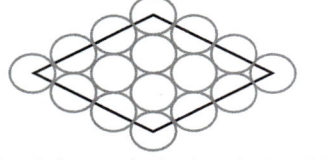

   .... cm

7. The area of a right-angled triangle is 1002.5cm^2. The length of its base is 0.4m. What is its height correct to two decimal places?

   .... cm

8. How many pairs of parallel sides are there in all the 2D shapes shown below?

   ....

9. What is the area of the shape below to the nearest 10cm^2?

   (Diagram not to scale)
   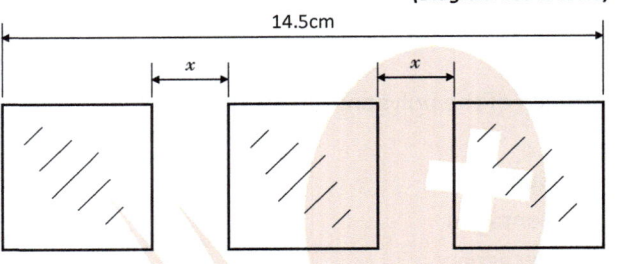

   .... cm^2

10. Three identical, square photos are shown below. Each photo has an area of 1369mm^2. What is the length of x?

    (Diagram not to scale)

    .... cm

11. Reflect the image below in line M to form a four digit number. What is the result of multiplying this number by 1.6 and subtracting 236.7 from the result?

    ....

12. A square is shown below along with four identical circles. The corner points of the square are at the centre points of each circle. The diameter of each circle is 0.0056km. What is the sum of the perimeters of 47 squares identical to the one shown below?

    .... cm

13. What is the median area of the three shapes below?

    (Diagram not to scale)
    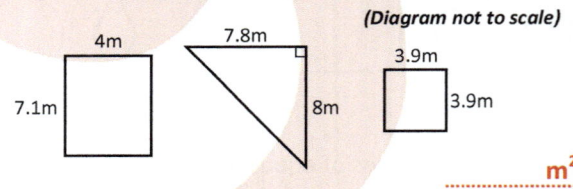

    .... m^2

14. A rectangle has a height of 12cm. The area of the rectangle is four times the area of a square of perimeter 36cm. What is the length of the rectangle?

    .... cm

15. If a rectangle, trapezium, regular decagon and an isosceles triangle are on a table, which statement below is false?
    a. 75% of the shapes are polygons.
    b. Quadrilateral to non quadrilateral ratio is 1:1.
    c. The perimeter of the decagon is equal to the sum of four of its side lengths multiplied by 2.5.

    ....

3D Shapes and Volume

3D Shapes and Volumes - Beginner

1. What is the name of the 3D shape below?

   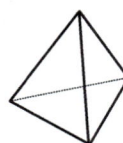

   ....

2. How many faces does a triangular prism have?

   ....

3. What is the name of the 3D shape below?

   ....

4. How many edges does a cube have?

   ....

5. How many vertices does the shape below have?

   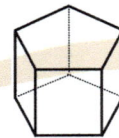

   ....

6. What 3D shape is formed when the net below is folded up?

   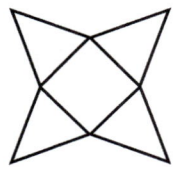

   ....

7. The net below forms a cuboid when folded up. What is the height of the cuboid?

   (Diagram not to scale)

   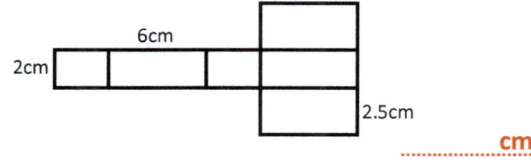

   .... cm

8. What 3D shape is formed when the net below is folded up?

   ....

9. A metal tank is 9 metres in length, 4 metres in width and 3 metres in height. What is its volume?

   .... m³

10. The volume of a cube is 64cm³. What is the length of the cube?

    .... cm

11. The volume of a cube is 100cm³. What is the total volume of 5 such cubes?

    .... cm³

12. The volume of the cuboid below is 90cm³. What is the volume of one of the cubes that make up the cuboid?

    .... cm³

13. What is the volume of the block below?

    (Diagram not to scale)

    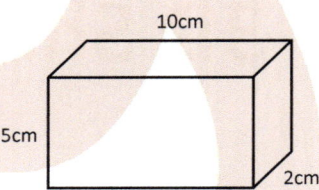

    .... cm³

14. The dimensions of two cuboids are shown below. Which cuboid has the larger volume?

    a. Length 4cm, width 9cm, height 4cm
    b. Length 5cm, width 12cm, height 2cm

    ....

15. Cube A has a volume of 60m³. The volume of cube B is a third of the volume of cube A. What is the combined volume of both cubes?

    .... m³

3D Shapes and Volumes - Intermediate

1. How many pairs of parallel faces does a hexagonal prism have?

   ....

2. What is the difference between the number of vertices of a tetrahedron and an octahedron?

   ....

3. What is the combined number of edges of the three shapes below?

   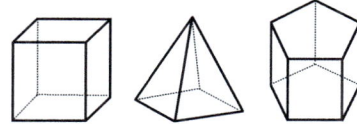

   ....

4. Name one 3D shape which has half as many faces as an octagonal prism.

   ....

5. Mike has 36 identical spheres that he puts into boxes 1 and 2 in the ratio of 2:1. How many hemispheres make up the spheres contained in box 1?

   ....

6. The net below forms a triangular prism. What is the length of the prism in metres to the nearest 10 metres?

   (Diagram not to scale)

   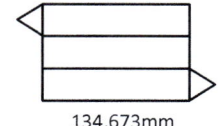

   134,673mm

   .... m

7. Elaine wants to create the nets for 24 identical cubes out of paper. She has 57 square faces already that can be used to create the nets. How many more square faces will she require to complete the 24 cube nets?

   ....

8. The net below when folded up forms a cube. Which face is parallel to the base when the cube is formed?

   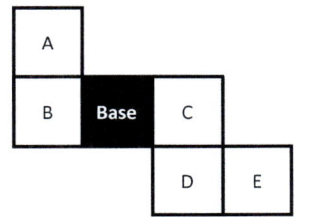

   ....

9. What is the volume of a cuboid with length 11cm, width 6cm and height 0.2m?

   .... cm³

10. The volume of a cube is 343m³. What is the area of one square face on the cube?

    .... m²

11. What is the volume of the triangular-shaped wedge shown below?

    (Diagram not to scale)

    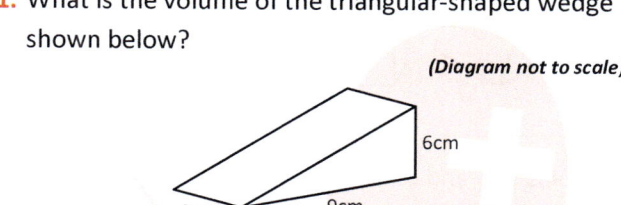

    .... cm³

12. The volume of a cuboid is 168m³. Its width is 7m and its height is 8m. What is its length?

    .... m

13. The volume of the cuboid below is 140m³. What is the area of face A?

    (Diagram not to scale)

    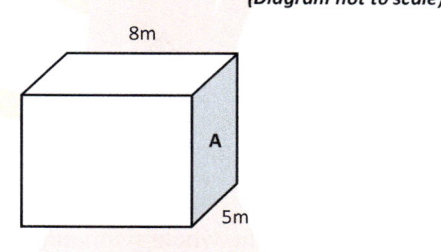

    .... m²

14. What is the volume of the swimming pool below?

    (Diagram not to scale)

    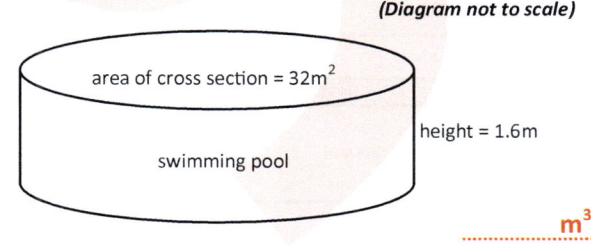

    .... m³

15. The cuboid shown below has its dimensions expressed in Roman numerals. What is its volume?

    (Diagram not to scale)

    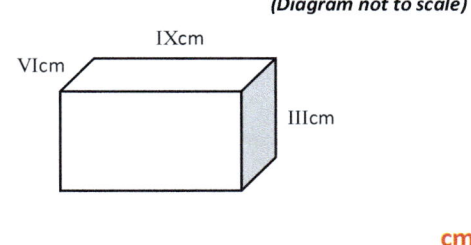

    .... cm³

3D Shapes and Volumes - Advanced

1. In total, how many edges are there in 3 tetrahedrons, 3 octagonal prisms and 1 square-based pyramid?

2. What is the sum of all the interior angles on all faces of a regular pentagonal prism?

   ....°

3. Based on all the shapes below, what is the mean number of vertices to two decimal places?

   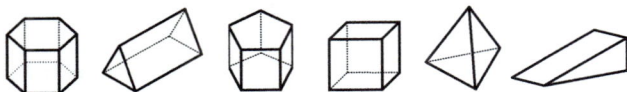

4. Cuboids A, B and C have the following dimensions. What is a simplified expression for the combined volumes of cuboids A, B and C? Assume units are all the same.

   Cuboid A: length = x, width = y, height = z

   Cuboid B: length = $x - 1$, width = x, height = 1

   Cuboid C: length = $x + 1$, width = x, height = 2

5. How many shapes below do not have a square or cube number of edges?

   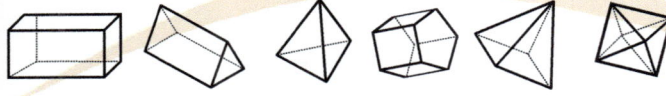

6. The volume of the whole swimming pool below is 31.6m³. What is the volume of the part of the swimming pool that contains water?

   (Diagram not to scale)

   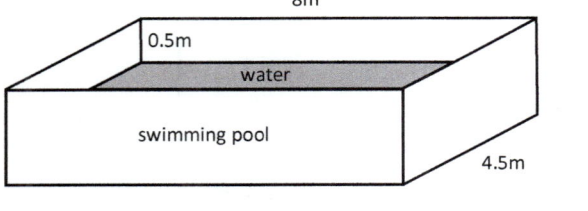

   .... m³

7. What is the volume of a cuboid in cubic centimetres with length 1.8cm, width 0.052m and height 60mm?

   .... cm³

8. The combined perimeters of two opposite faces of a cube is 112cm. What is the volume of the cube?

   .... cm³

9. How many times larger is the volume of the box compared to the volume of the sphere?

   (Diagram not to scale)

   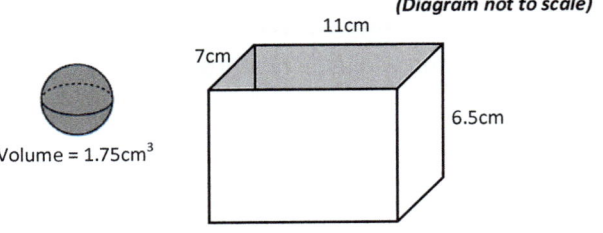

   Volume = 1.75cm³

   ....

10. What is the volume of the shape below?

    (Diagram not to scale)

    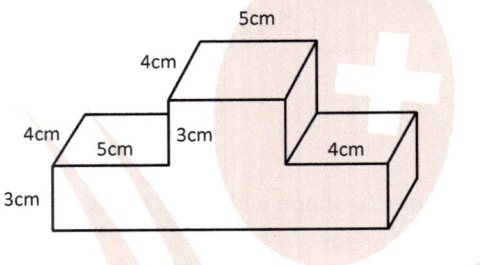

    .... cm³

11. Find the volume of the cuboid below, given that each small cube is 4.73cm³ in volume.

    .... cm³

12. The volume of a cube is 32.9cm³. The volume of a tetrahedron is 19.1cm³. What is the combined volume of 3 identical cubes and 6 identical tetrahedrons?

    .... cm³

13. The volume of the metal ingot below is the product of the area of face E and the length. The cross section of face E is shown below. What is the volume of the ingot?

    (Diagrams not to scale)

    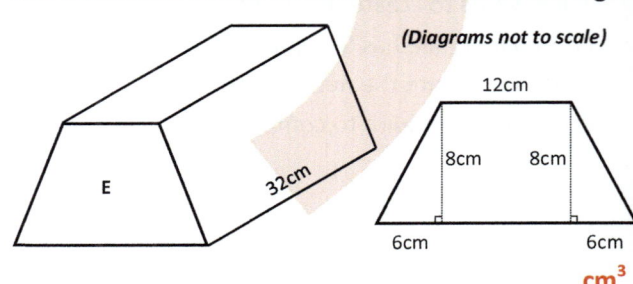

    .... cm³

14. The volume of a cuboid is 256cm³. Its length is 4cm and its height is 16cm. What is its width in millimetres, expressed in Roman numerals?

    .... mm

15. The length of a cuboid is 12cm. Its width is 4.5 times its length and its height is 45% of its length. What is the volume of the cuboid?

    .... cm³

Probability

Probability - Beginner

Answer questions 1 to 5 by choosing one of the probabilities on the scale below.

How likely are the following?

1. The month of August directly follows the month of July.

   ....

2. You roll a fair die and it lands on 4, 5 or 6.

   ....

3. It will snow for 20 consecutive days in London in a year.

   ....

4. The temperature will reach 25°C on at least one day in August in England.

   ....

5. A square has five sides which are equal in length.

   ....

6. Pauline has the following six triangles with numbers on them in her pocket. She selects one at random. What is the probability that the triangle has a number on it which is greater than 6? Give your answer as a fraction.

   ....

7. Emma tosses a fair coin. What is the probability that it does not show a head? Give your answer as a decimal.

   ....

8. What is the probability that the spinner below lands on a white segment? Give your answer as a fraction.

   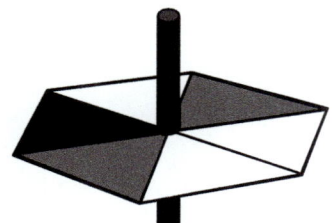

   ....

9. If today is the 4th of January, what is the probability that tomorrow is the 8th of January?

   ....

10. A fair six-sided die is rolled. What is the probability that it lands face up on an odd number which is not 1 or 3? Give your answer as a fraction.

    ....

11. Pinky selects a numbered disc at random from the bag below. What is the probability that the disc has a 4 on it? Give your answer as a fraction.

    ....

12. 25% of the pencils in a pencil case are broken. What is the probability that a pencil chosen at random from the case is not broken? Express your answer as a fraction.

    ....

13. The letters below are placed in a folder. What is the probability of selecting one letter at random that is an A? Give your answer as a fraction.

    ....

14. A card is selected at random from a standard pack of 52 playing cards. What is the probability that it is from the hearts suit? Give your answer as a fraction.

    ....

15. A square is chosen at random from those shown below. What is the probability that it is shaded? Give your answer as a fraction.

    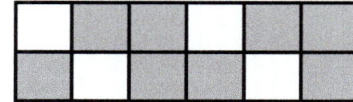

    ....

Probability - Intermediate

Answer questions 1 to 5 by choosing one of the probabilities on the scale below.

|---|---|---|---|---|
| Impossible | Unlikely | Even Chance | Likely | Certain |

How likely are the following?

1. A subject chosen at random from history, sociology, computing and science contains at least one letter 'o' in its name.

   ....

2. A fair coin is tossed 10 times and only tails are recorded.

   ....

3. If today is Monday 14th and last Monday was the 7th, then a week from tomorrow will be the 22nd.

   ....

4. Adam has eight monetary notes in his pocket; two £10 notes, two £5 notes, two £50 notes and two £20 notes. He selects one at random, and it is worth more than £10.

   ....

5. If a day is to be chosen from next week, how likely is it that its duration will be 730 minutes?

   ....

6. Mia selects a numbered disc at random from those shown below. What is the probability that the number is exactly divisible by 2 and 3? Give your answer as a fraction.

   32, 33, 34, 35, 36, 37, 38, 39, 40, 41, 42, 43

   ....

7. A card is selected at random from a standard pack of 52 playing cards. What is the probability that it is black and either an ace, a three or a queen? Give your answer as a fraction in its lowest terms.

   ....

8. The probability of rain on any given day in a certain city is 45%. On how many days of the next 40, should the city expect some rain?

   .... days

9. A box contains three 50 pence coins, five 20 pence coins and a dozen £2 coins. What is the probability that a coin chosen at random is circular? Give your answer as a fraction.

   ....

10. The table below shows summarised test mark information for a set of students. What is the probability that a student selected at random scored between 10 and 30 on the test? Give your answer as a fraction.

Marks	Number of students
10 to 20	2
21 to 30	8
31 to 40	10
41 to 50	9
51 to 60	3

    ....

11. Elia selects a month of the year at random. What is the probability that it contains less than 31 days? Give your answer as a fraction.

    ....

12. A value is selected at random from the grid below. What is the probability that the value is a triangular number? Give your answer as a fraction.

1	2	3	4	5
6	7	8	9	10
11	12	13	14	15
16	17	18	19	20
21	22	23	24	25

    ....

13. A fair die is rolled. What is the probability that it lands face up on a value which is equivalent to the Roman numerals of II or VI? Give your answer as a fraction.

    ....

14. A square is selected at random from the grid below. What is the probability that the square contains a smiley face? Give your answer as a fraction.

    ....

15. What is the probability that the spinner lands on a number which is greater than 3? Give your answer as a fraction.

    Spinner values: 19, 3, 1, 95, 64, 21

    ....

Probability - Advanced

1. Gail tosses six fair coins. What is the probability that all six coins land heads up? Give your answer as a fraction.

    ....

2. A room contains 174 DVDs, 360 print cartridges, 38 fans, 209 pads and 19 pictures. One of these objects is selected at random from the room. Expressed as a percentage, what is the probability that it is a print cartridge?

    .... %

3. Zak rolls the two fair spinners below. What is the probability that the spinner on the left will show a cube number and the spinner on the right will show a number greater than 9.76? Give your answer as a fraction.

    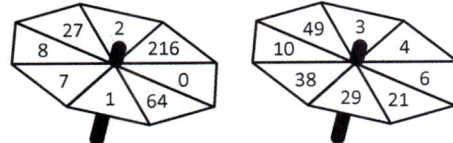

    ....

4. Claire adds the following four cards to a standard pack of 52 playing cards. She removes one card at random from the newly formed pack. What is the probability that it is a black card with a value between 3 and 8, inclusive of both values? Give your answer as a fraction.

    ....

5. The probability of a chair with four legs being green in colour is $2/5$ and the probability of a chair with three legs being green in colour is $1/6$. In a warehouse, there are 15 chairs with four legs and 18 chairs with three legs. How many legs in total would you expect to find on green chairs in the warehouse?

    ....

6. A fair die is rolled 207 times. How many times would you expect to obtain a value of less than 5?

    ....

7. The vehicles below were recorded passing down a street over a five minute interval. What is the probability that two vehicles selected at random (with replacement) are a car followed by a van? Give your answer as a fraction.

Vehicle	Number of vehicles
Car	78
Van	18
Lorry	9
Bus	16
Taxi	5

8. A game consists of selecting a ball at random from a bag and noting what you score. The bag contains 20 balls. Three of the balls are worth 16 points, eight are worth 23 points, four are worth 13 points and five worth 14 points. What is the probability that the ball drawn out will be worth more than the mean score of all 20 balls? Give your answer as a fraction.

    ....

9. The probability that a team wins a game of netball is $2/15$ and the probability of a draw is $2/5$. The only other outcome is a loss for the team. What is the probability that the team loses the game? Give your answer as a fraction.

    ....

10. Ernie has two boxes of balls. He selects one ball at random from each box. What is the probability that they are both shaded? Give your answer as a fraction.

    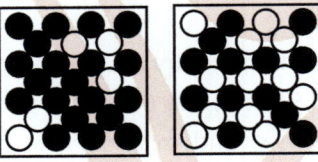

    ....

11. What is the probability that the spinner lands on a grey or black section when spun? Give your answer as a fraction.

    ....

12. The letters in the word below are shuffled and three are chosen at random, without replacement. What is the probability that the three Ls are selected? Give your answer as a fraction.

    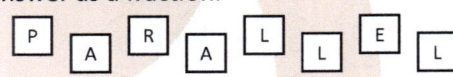

    ....

13. Two fair dice are rolled. What is the probability of throwing a two or less with the first die and a three or more with the second die?

    ....

14. A box contains 150 paper clips of which 22% are red, 36% are yellow and the rest are blue. All 150 paper clips are taken out of the box. How many blue paper clips would you expect to find?

    ....

15. A fair die and fair coin are both thrown. What is the probability that the coin shows a tail and the die shows an even number? Give your answer as a fraction.

    ....

Coordinates and Transformations

Coordinates and Transformations - Beginner

1. A straight line lies between coordinates (2, 2) and (6, 2). What are the coordinates of the midpoint of the line?

   (_ , _)

2. What are the coordinates of point K on the grid below?

   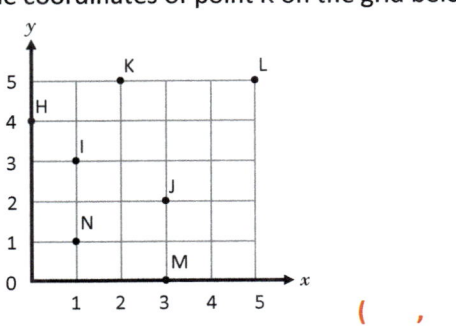

   (_ , _)

3. What are the coordinates of the centre of the circle below?

   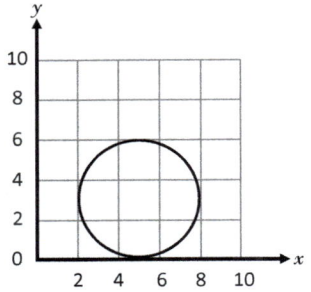

   (_ , _)

4. Three corner points of a rectangle are shown below. What are the coordinates of the last corner point?

   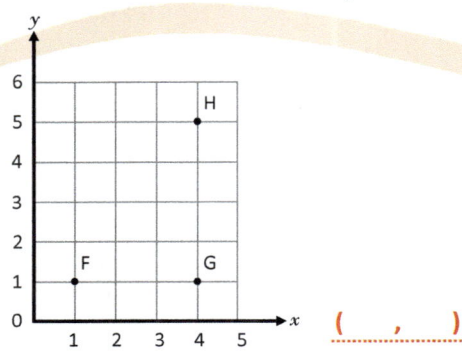

   (_ , _)

5. A straight line goes through coordinates (-2, -2), (1, 1) and (5, 5). Will it also pass through coordinates (0, 0)?

   _____

6. The points (4, 6), (5, 4), (4, 2) and (3, 4) are plotted on a grid and joined up in order using straight lines. What object is formed?

   _____

7. At what coordinates is the treasure on the grid below?

   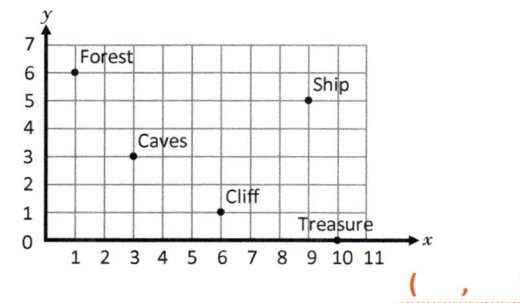

   (_ , _)

8. Point A at coordinates (0, 4) is translated down by two units. What are its new coordinates?

   (_ , _)

9. The museum on the grid below is translated left three squares and up one square. What are its new coordinates?

   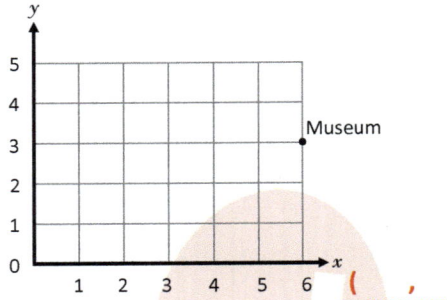

   (_ , _)

10. The triangle on the grid below is translated four squares right and two squares down. What are the new coordinates of corner point P?

    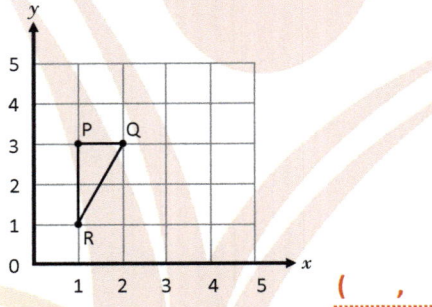

    (_ , _)

11. Point B at coordinates (-1, 3) is reflected in the y-axis. What are the new coordinates of point B?

    (_ , _)

12. Trapezium T is to be reflected in the line $x = 3$. What will be the new coordinates of point C?

    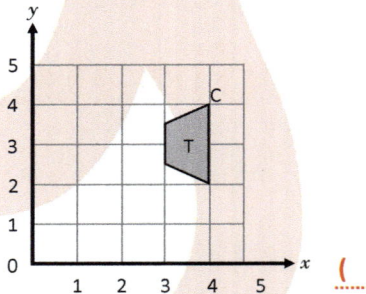

    (_ , _)

13. Point H at coordinates (3, 1) is reflected in the line at $y = 2$ and then translated down one unit. What are the new coordinates of point H?

    (_ , _)

14. Point W at coordinates (0, 1) is rotated 90° clockwise about point (0, 0). What are the new coordinates of point W?

    (_ , _)

15. Which letter (A to E) below shows the line L rotated 180° anticlockwise about its centre? Circle your answer.

    L   A   B   C   D   E

Coordinates and Transformations - Intermediate

1. What are the coordinates of the midpoint of the line on the grid below?

   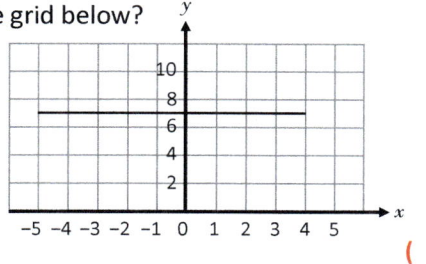

   (,)

2. Which lettered point below is at coordinates (-3, 2)?

   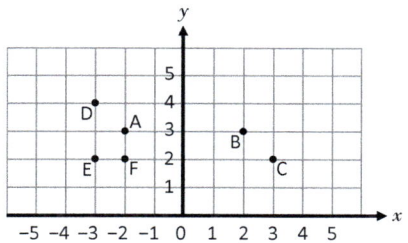

   ....

3. Three corner coordinates of a parallelogram are at (1, 5), (3, 5) and (0, 0). What are the coordinates of the last corner of the parallelogram, given that its x-coordinate is less than zero?

   (,)

4. What are the coordinates of the chemist?

   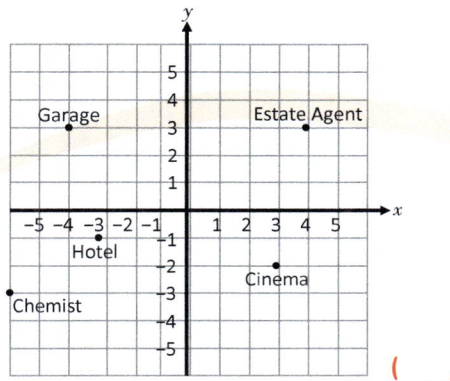

   (,)

5. What are the centre point coordinates of a square with corner points at (1, 1), (7, 1), (7, -5) and (1, -5)?

   (,)

6. What are the coordinates of point Q below?

   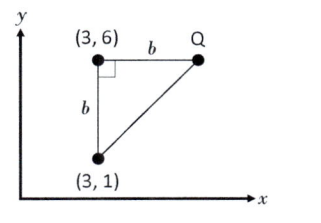

   (,)

7. Point G at coordinates (0, 2) is translated 3 squares down, 5 squares right and 3 squares down. What are the new coordinates of point G?

   (,)

8. A point V has y-coordinate 14. Its x-coordinate is 4 units higher than -13. Point V is translated 6 units up. What are the new coordinates of point V?

   (,)

9. What are the coordinates of the lettered point which is directly east of point S on the grid below?

   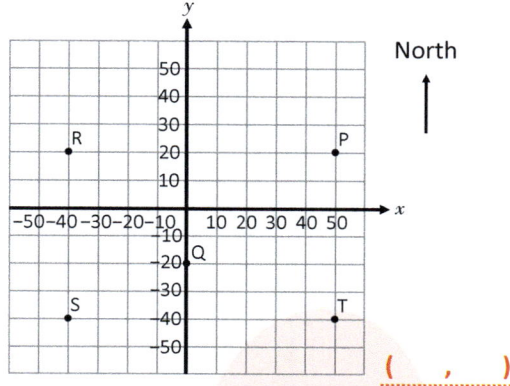

   (,)

10. The line PQ is to be translated 13.45 units left. What will be the new coordinates of point P?

    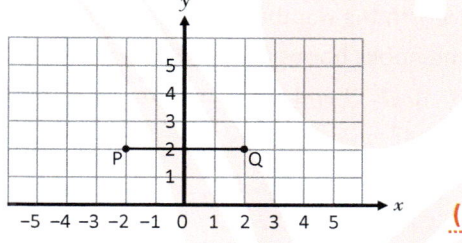

    (,)

11. Point Q at coordinates (0.5, -0.17) is reflected in the y-axis. What are the new coordinates of point Q?

    (,)

12. Triangle T below is reflected in line M. What are the new coordinates of point C?

    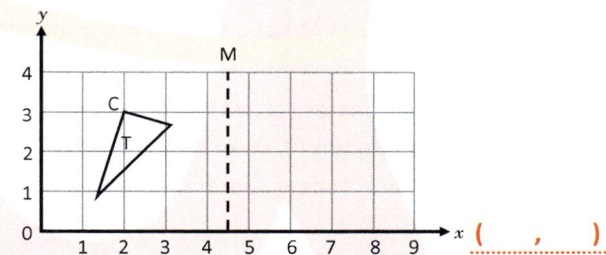

    (,)

13. Which of lines L1 to L6 would point P need to be reflected in to move it to point Q?

    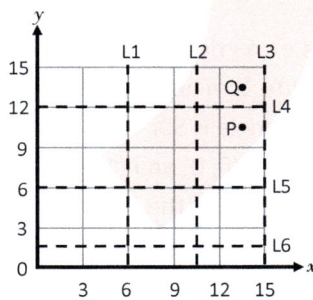

    ....

14. Point R at coordinates (-1, -3) is rotated 90° clockwise about point (0, 0). What are the new coordinates of point R?

    (,)

15. Point Z at coordinates (1, 1) is rotated three right angles anticlockwise about (0, 0). What are the new coordinates of point Z?

    (,)

Coordinates and Transformations - Advanced

1. What are the coordinates of the labelled point directly northwest of the building at coordinates (-√9, -(2²))?

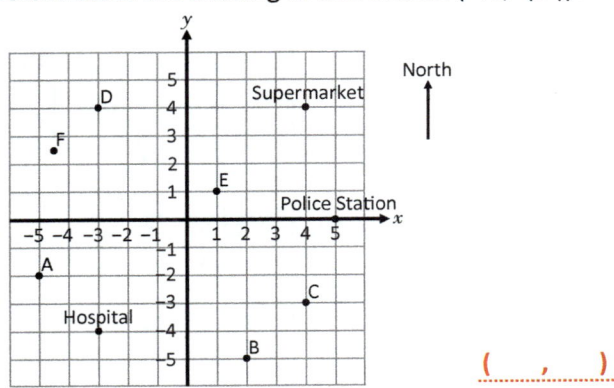

   (......, ...)

2. Harin is playing a game of throwing rubber hoops onto the targets on the grid below. Hooking a hoop around a target is worth the number of points on the grid. While playing, he hooks hoops at coordinates (2, 0), (-4, 1), (-5, 3), (3, 3), (2, 0) and (1, 4). How many points does he score in total?

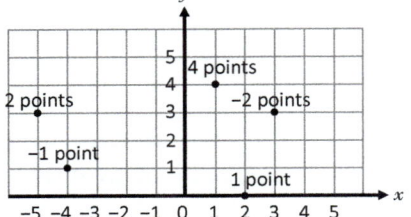

   .... points

3. Point A is at coordinates (-3, 0). It is reflected in the y-axis and then translated 3 units down before being reflected in the x-axis. What are its new coordinates?

   (......, ...)

4. Point Z is at coordinates (16, 34). It is rotated 180° clockwise around point (0, 0) and then translated 40 units up. What are its new coordinates?

   (......, ...)

5. Point J at coordinates (0.63, 0.09) is translated 1.56 units left and 0.93 units down. What are its new coordinates?

   (......, ...)

6. A rectangle is on a grid and the units of each square on the grid measure 1cm horizontally by 1cm vertically. The area of the rectangle is 50cm². Two of its corner points are at coordinates (0, 0) and (10, 0). What are the possible coordinates of the other corner points of the rectangle?

   (......, ...) and (......, ...) or (......, ...) and (......, ...)

7. A triangle has corner coordinates at points A (-2, -4), B (3, -4) and C (2 + 1⁴, √49). The triangle is reflected in the line $x = 4$. What are the new coordinates of point C?

   (......, ...)

Using the grid below, answer questions 8 to 11.

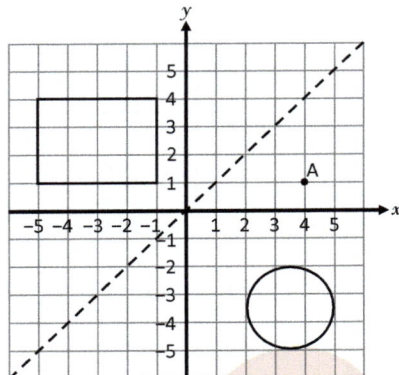

8. Point A is rotated 90° clockwise about point (3, -2). What are the new coordinates of point A?

   (......, ...)

9. The rectangle is rotated 90° anticlockwise about point (-1, 1). The circle is translated left 3 squares and up 1.5 squares. At which coordinates do the two shapes touch after the transformations?

   (......, ...)

10. The rectangle is reflected in the dashed line. What are the new coordinates of the centre of the rectangle?

    (......, ...)

11. What is the translation that maps point A onto the centre coordinates of the circle?

    (......)

12. Jan is standing at coordinates (-20,-20). She is facing the point -20 on the x-axis. She turns through 270° clockwise and walks for 5 units. What coordinate will she be standing at now?

    (......, ...)

13. Point M is at coordinates (12, 2). It is rotated 90° anticlockwise about point (0, 0). It is then translated 7 units down before being reflected in the x-axis. What are the new coordinates of point M?

    (......, ...)

14. Miss Smith digs at coordinates (-8, 0), (4, 10), (-6, 4) and (-8, 8) on the grid below. The grid represents a beach with buried money. How much money does she find in total?

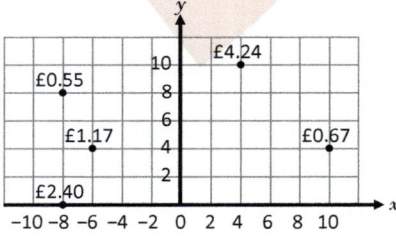

    £ ....

15. Point N at coordinates (-1.35, 0.75) is translated 3 units right. It is then reflected in the y-axis. What are its new coordinates?

    (......, ...)

FIRST PAST THE POST®

Answers & Explanations

Mathematics:
Worded Problems

Standard Format
Book 2

Four Operations - Beginner, page 2

Question	Answer	Explanation
1	322	267 + 55 = **322**
2	455	838 − 383 = **455**
3	14	The completed grid should look like this: ? = **14** | 8	7	9	→ 24 | **14**	7	3	→ 24 | 2	10	12	→ 24 ↓ ↓ ↓ 24 24 24
4	£84	30 × £2.80 = 3 × 10 × £2.80 = 3 × £28 = **£84**
5	£405	Cost of one lawnmower = £2700 ÷ 20 = £270 ÷ 2 = £135. Therefore, the cost of three lawnmowers = 3 × £135 = **£405**.
6	7	(A × A) + (B × B) = 130 $A^2 + 9^2 = 130$ → $A^2 + 81 = 130$ → $A^2 = 130 - 81$ → $A^2 = 49$ Therefore, A = √49 = **7**.
7	18	Creating an equation from the worded statement gives: 100N ÷ 60 = 30 → 10N ÷ 6 = 30 → 5N ÷ 3 = 30 → 5N = 3 × 30 → 5N = 90 Therefore, N = 90 ÷ 5 = **18**.
8	256	The completed pyramid should look like this: ? = **256** 256 8 32 2 4 8 1 2 2 4
9	234g	As £3.60 = 360p, number of 10p coins in bag = 360p ÷ 10p = 36. As each coin weighs 6.5g, 36 coins weigh 36 × 6.5g = **234g**.
10	65ml	Number of bottles in crate = 10 × 100 = 1,000. One bottle contains 65,000ml ÷ 1,000 = **65ml**.
11	118	Use BIDMAS: 83 − 8 × 7 + 91 = 83 − 56 + 91 = 174 − 56 = **118**
12	960cm	Length of carpet (L) = 360cm. Width of carpet (W) = L ÷ 3 = 360cm ÷ 3 = 120cm. Perimeter = 2L + 2W = (2 × 360cm) + (2 × 120cm) = 720cm + 240cm = **960cm**.
13	9	Let x be the missing number: 15x − 3 = 12x + 24 → 15x − 12x = 24 + 3 → 3x = 27 → x = **9**
14	140	Number of red counters in bag = $\frac{1}{3}$ of 240 = 240 ÷ 3 = 80. Number of counters in bag not coloured red = 240 − 80 = 160. Number of blue counters in bag = $\frac{1}{8}$ of 160 = 160 ÷ 8 = 20. Number of counters in bag that are neither red nor blue = 160 − 20 = **140**.
15	52	Use BIDMAS: (72 − 16) ÷ 8 + 5 × 9 = 56 ÷ 8 + 5 × 9 = 7 + 45 = **52**

Four Operations - Intermediate, page 3

Question	Answer	Explanation
1	0.6cm	7 × 462 = 3234mm = 3.234m Length of capping left over = 3.24m - 3.234m = 0.006m = **0.6cm**.
2	R = 8, S = −3	The completed grid should look like this: Each row and column adds up to 4. R = **8**, S = **-3** <table><tr><td>-7</td><td>10</td><td>1</td></tr><tr><td>8</td><td>-1</td><td>-3</td></tr><tr><td>3</td><td>-5</td><td>6</td></tr></table>
3	1,810mm	Length of shaded inset area = 57.4cm - 1.8cm - 1.8cm = 53.8cm = 538mm. Height of shaded inset area = 40.3cm - 1.8cm - 1.8cm = 36.7cm = 367mm. Perimeter of shaded inset area = (2 × 538mm) + (2 × 367mm) = 1,076mm + 734mm = **1,810mm**.
4	3	Creating an equation from the worded statement gives: $(65N - 7) \div 4 = 47 \rightarrow 65N - 7 = 188 \rightarrow 65N = 195 \rightarrow N = 195 \div 65 \rightarrow N = \mathbf{3}$
5	£53.35	Cost of CDs = 8 × £6.35 = £50.80. Cost of marker pens = (6 ÷ 2) × 85p = £2.55. Total cost = £50.80 + £2.55 = **£53.35**.
6	-216	The completed pyramid should look like this: ? = **−216** −216 6 −36 −2 −3 12 −2 1 −3 −4
7	421	As $\frac{1}{3}$ are sitting upstairs there must be $1 - \frac{1}{3} = \frac{2}{3}$ sitting downstairs. $\frac{2}{3}$ of 2,526 = (2 × 2,526) ÷ 3 = 5,052 ÷ 3 = 1,684 people downstairs. As $\frac{3}{4}$ are adults there must be $1 - \frac{3}{4} = \frac{1}{4}$ that are children. $\frac{1}{4}$ of 1,684 = 1,684 ÷ 4 = **421**
8	391	Total score from three darts = 17 + (2 × 18) + (3 × 19) = 17 + 36 + 57 = 110. New lower number = 501 − 110 = **391**.
9	2	$\frac{5}{8}$ of 48 = 5 × 6 = 30. $\frac{2}{3}$ of 48 = 2 × 16 = 32. Difference = 32 − 30 = **2**.
10	£9,486	Car price paid is £8,560 − (£8,560 ÷ 16) = £8,560 − £535 = £8,025. Total price paid = £8,025 + £521 (for Satellite Navigation) + £940 (for Park Assist) = **£9,486**.
11	30,151	Use BIDMAS: (81 + (−9)) x 2 + 30,007 = 72 × 2 + 30,007 = 144 + 30,007 = **30,151**
12	−60	Equation 2: 42 ÷ 6 − C = 11 → 7 − C = 11 → C = −4. Now, substitute C = −4. Equation 1: 7 × −8 + (−4) = R → −56 − 4 = R → R = **−60**.
13	−19	A = 17 + (8 × 3) − 3 = 17 + 24 − 3 = 38. B = −8 + (21 ÷ 7) + 3 = −8 + 3 + 3 = −2. A ÷ B = 38 ÷ −2 = **−19**.
14	£27.60	Method 1: Pay £360. Method 2: £42 + (24 × £14.40) = £42 + £345.60 = £387.60. Difference in payment methods = £387.60 − £360 = **£27.60**.
15	17	Use BIDMAS: −12 + (4 × 7) − (−4) + (18 ÷ 3) + (−9) = −12 + 28 + 4 + 6 − 9 = **17**

Four Operations - Advanced, page 4

Question	Answer	Explanation
1	£48.42	Sum of five items = £12.35 + £7.50 + £10.72 + £16.93 + £4.67 = £52.17. Applying '75p off for every £10 spent', total amount to deduct is 5 × 75p = £3.75. Therefore, total amount Fabia pays is £52.17 – £3.75 = **£48.42**.
2	P = –9 Q = –2.6	Bottom row sum = 3.6 + (–6.2) + (–5.4) = 3.6 – 6.2 – 5.4 = 3.6 – 11.6 = –8. From top row: P + (–6) + 7 = –8 → P = 6 – 15 → P = **–9** From left column: –9 + Q + 3.6 = –8 → Q = –8 + 9 – 3.6 → Q = **–2.6**
3	R = 4.2	From middle column: –6 + R + (–6.2) = –8 → R = –8 + 6 + 6.2 → R = **4.2**
4	S = –9.6	From right column: 7 + S + (–5.4) = –8 → S = –8 – 7 + 5.4 → S = **–9.6**
5	(a) 3,444 miles (b) 8 hrs	(a) London to New York distance = 5,545 ÷ 1.61 = **3,444 miles**. (b) As New York is 5 hours behind London time, 12.30pm London time is 7.30am New York time. Flight time is from 7.30am to 3.30pm i.e. **8 hrs**.
6	7.5 – (–12) – 3.5 x (4 + 1)	Brackets should be inserted around the 4 + 1 to create an answer of 2: 7.5 – (–12) – 3.5 × **(4 + 1)** = 7.5 + 12 – 3.5 × 5 = 19.5 – 17.5 = **2**
7	–22.28	The completed pyramid should look like this: ? = **–22.28** –22.28 –6.75 3.3 4.5 –1.5 –2.2 –3 –1.5 1 –2.2
8	2	(–48 ÷ (–4 + (–0.4) – 3.6) – 3^3 + 5 × 5.2) ÷ 2.5 = (–48 ÷ –8 – 27 + 5 × 5.2) ÷ 2.5 = (6 – 27 + 5 × 5.2) ÷ 2.5 = (6 – 27 + 26) ÷ 2.5 = 5 ÷ 2.5 = **2**
9	(a) 52cm (b) 12cm²	(a) Whole shape perimeter = (2 × 18cm) + (2 × 5cm) + (18cm ÷ 3) = **52cm**. (b) Triangle area = $^1/_2$ (b × h) = $^1/_2$ (6cm × (22cm – 18cm)) = **12cm²**.
10	3.4	Lara's 1st result: 7th square number (49) × 6th prime number (13) = 637. Lara's 2nd result: 6th cube number (216) – 7th triangular number (28) = 188. 1st result ÷ 2nd result = 637 ÷ 188 = 3.38829... = **3.4** to the nearest tenth.
11	661,527	As (N ÷ 9) = 8,167, N = 9 × 8,167 = 73,503. As N should have been × by 9, Sean's answer should have been 73,503 × 9 = **661,527**.
12	104	Kim has read $^4/_7$ of 364 pages i.e. (4 × 364) ÷ 7 = 1,456 ÷ 7 = 208 pages. $^6/_7$ of 364 pages is (6 × 364) ÷ 7 = 2,184 ÷ 7 = 312 pages. Kim has yet to read 312 – 208 = **104** pages.
13	9	12 of the 13 (119cm) planks required can be cut from four 3,580mm planks. 8 of the 9 (160cm) planks required can be cut from four 3,580mm planks. The 13th (119cm) plank and the ninth (160cm) plank can be cut from one more 3,580mm plank. Total number of 3580mm planks required = 4 + 4 + 1 = **9**.
14	2.625	Total number of slices sold = £82.80 ÷ 72p = 8280p ÷ 72p = 115. Number of slices left unsold = (17 × 8) – 115 = 21. Number of pizzas unsold = 21 ÷ 8 = **2.625**.
15	1,314kg	Car (1.25 tonnes): 1.25 × 1,000kg = 1,250kg Tanya (10 stone): 10 × 6.35kg = 63.5kg Total = 1,250kg + 63.5kg = 1,313.5kg = **1,314kg** to the nearest kg.

Number Values and Number Sequences - Beginner, page 6

Question	Answer	Explanation
1	**3,459**	Three thousand four hundred and fifty-nine = 3 thousand + 4 hundred + 5 tens + 9 units = 3,000 + 400 + 50 + 9 = **3,459**
2	**Twenty-four thousand six hundred and fifteen**	24,615 = 20,000 + 4,000 + 600 + 10 + 5 = 24 thousand + 6 hundred + 1 ten + 5 units, giving **Twenty-four thousand six hundred and fifteen**.
3	**78,738, 78,387, 77,883, 77,838, 77,807**	Numbers in descending order are: **78,738, 78,387, 77,883, 77,838, 77,807**
4	**18,000ml**	Water in container 1 is 20,007ml. Water in container 2 is 2,007ml. Difference = 20,007ml − 2,007ml = **18,000ml**
5	**£80**	Cost of washing machine is £384.50. As the 8 in the price is in the tens column, the 8 is worth 8 tens i.e. **£80**.
6	**4,000**	In the number breakdown: 14,327 = 10,000 + N + 300 + 20 + 7, the N is in the thousands column and therefore worth **4,000**.
7	**11kg**	As 10.63kg is closer to 11kg than 10kg, the weight is **11kg** to the nearest kg.
8	**16 thousands**	160 hundreds = 160 × 100 = 16,000 which is **16 thousands**.
9	**32**	The number of squares in each pattern sequence is: 3, 4, 5, 6, 7, 8, 9... As one square is made up of 4 matchsticks, the number of matchsticks in each pattern sequence is: 12, 16, 20, 24, 28, **32**, 36... Number of matchsticks in 6th term (shown in bold above) is **32**.
10	**56**	As n^{th} term rule is $7n$, 3rd term value = 7(3) = 7 × 3 = 21 and 5th term value = 7(5) = 7 × 5 = 35. 3rd term + 5th term = 21 + 35 = **56**.
11	**$4n$**	As difference between patterns is +4, use $4n$ where n is the term number. Test rule: For pattern 1, $4n$ = 4 × 1 = 4 circles; for pattern 2, $4n$ = 4 × 2 = 8 circles; for pattern 3, $4n$ = 4 × 3 = 12 circles, etc. Answers match sequence numbers. Rule is therefore **$4n$**.
12	**0**	As the difference between the terms is +8, the missing 2nd term must be the 1st term + 8 or the 3rd term - 8. Term 1 + 8 = − 8 + 8 = 0; Term 3 − 8 = 8 − 8 = 0. Therefore, the missing 2nd term is **0**.
13	**$n + 7$**	As the difference between terms is +1, use $1n$ where n is the term number. To find the first term of 8, $1n$ + ? = 8 where n = 1 and ? = 7 to balance the equation 1 + 7 = 8. Rule is therefore $1n + 7$ or simply **$n + 7$**.
14	**38**	The pattern sequence is 1, 4, 7, 10, 13, **16**, 19, **22**... with a difference of +3 between adjacent terms. Sum of the number of circles in patterns 6 and 8 is therefore 16 + 22 = **38**.
15	**8.1**	The difference between adjacent known terms in the sequence 'A, 4.02, 4.05, 4.08, B' is 0.03. Therefore, missing term A = 4.02 − 0.03 = 3.99 and missing term B = 4.08 + 0.03 = 4.11. Sum of missing terms = 3.99 + 4.11 = **8.1**.

Number Values and Number Sequences - Intermediate, page 7

Question	Answer	Explanation
1	Seven hundred and thirty-four thousand six hundred and one	734,601 = 700,000 + 30,000 + 4000 + 600 + 0 + 1 = (700 thousand + 30 thousand + 4 thousand) + 6 hundred + 0 tens + 1 unit, giving **seven hundred and thirty-four thousand six hundred and one**.
2	3,002,374	Three million two thousand three hundred and seventy-four = 3,000,000 + 2,000 + 300 + 70 + 4 = **3,002,374**
3	7,400	Descending: 227,802, 227,207, 227,028, 220,782, 219,807, 218,782, 218,728 Of the seven numbers, 227,207 is the 2nd largest and 219,807 the 5th largest. Difference = 227,207 − 219,807 = **7,400**.
4	607,030	4$\underline{7}$,286 → 7 worth 7,000, 9,1$\underline{3}$8 → 3 worth 30, $\underline{6}$54,279 → 6 worth 600,000 Sum = 7,000 + 30 + 600,000 = **607,030**.
5	£499	Television A cost (£196.27) rounded to the nearest £10 is £200. Television B cost (£298.74) rounded to the nearest pound (£) is £299. Sum of rounded costs = £200 + £299 = **£499**.
6	403.210	In the number 403.2095, the 4dp is 5. As this number is ≥ 5, the 3dp 9, is increased by one. This gives **403.210** to 3dp.
7	£15,000	Price of diamond ring is 10,000 × £1.54 = £15,400. As the 4 in the hundreds column is < 5, the price is rounded down to **£15,000** to the nearest £1,000.
8	59	The six patterns are a sequence of prime numbers: 2, 3, 5, 7, 11 and 13. Patterns 7, 8 and 9 must therefore have 17, 19 and 23 rectangles respectively. Total number of rectangles = 17 + 19 + 23 = **59**.
9	$5n + 2$	As the difference between the terms is +5, start with $5n$ where n is the term number. To find the 1st term of 7 we have $5n$ + ? = 7 where n = 1 for 1st term and ? = 2 to balance the equation 5(1) + 2 = 7. Rule is therefore **$5n + 2$**.
10	9	As n^{th} term rule is $3n - 2$, 4th term value = 3(4) − 2 = 12 − 2 = 10 and 7th term value = 3(7) − 2 = 21 − 2 = 19. 7th term − 4th term = 19 − 10 = **9**.
11	$5\,^5/_8$	In terms of eighths, the sequence is $^9/_8$, $^{18}/_8$, $^{27}/_8$, $^{36}/_8$, ?, $^{54}/_8$. Difference between terms is + $^9/_8$. The missing fifth term is ($^{36}/_8$) + ($^9/_8$) = $^{45}/_8$ = **$5\,^5/_8$**.
12	unshaded	Hexagon number required ÷ number of hexagons in pattern = 38 ÷ 8 = 4 remainder 6. The sixth hexagon on the fifth repeating pattern, (which is the 32 + 6 = 38th hexagon), is **unshaded**.
13	243	Working backwards from the sixth term value of 3 and multiplying by 3 gives the following descending sequence: 729, **243**, 81, 27, 9, 3. 2nd term = **243**.
14	A = 15 B = 12	Odd numbered terms are ascending even numbers starting at 2. Even numbered terms are ascending triangular numbers. Term A is the next triangular number after 10, which is **15**. Term B is the next even number after 10, which is **12**.
15	10, 20, 30, 40, 50, 60	Numbers rounded to the nearest 10 are: 54.85 is 50; 26.18 is 30; 35.63 is 40; 18.71 is 20; 10.42 is 10; 57.24 is 60. Ascending sequence is: **10, 20, 30, 40, 50, 60**.

Number Values and Number Sequences - Advanced, page 8

Question	Answer	Explanation
1	(a) 5,553,353, 5,553,053, 5,535,355, 5,535,335, 5,535,053, 5,335,335 (b) 17,718	(a) Numbers in descending order are: 5,553,353 5,553,053 5,535,355 5,535,335 5,535,053 5,335,335 (b) Difference between the 2nd and 4th largest numbers: 5,553,053 – 5,535,335 = **17,718**.
2	57,000,000	974,146 is closer to 1 million than to 900,000. So, 56,974,146 to the nearest 100,000 is **57,000,000.**
3	600,000 3,000,000 200,000,000	7<u>6</u>84321 → The 6 is in the hundred thousands column and worth **600,000**. 8<u>3</u>029705 → The 3 is in the millions column and worth **3,000,000**. <u>2</u>15408396 → The 2 is in the hundred millions column and worth **200,000,000**.
4	(a) 1,743,804 cu.ft. (b) 581,300 cu.ft.	(a) One million seven hundred and forty-three thousand eight hundred and four = 1,000,000 + 743,000 + 800 + 4 = **1,743,804 cubic feet**. (b) Air in one balloon = 1,743,804 cubic feet ÷ 3 = 581,268 cubic feet. 581,268 cubic feet rounded to the nearest 100 = **581,300 cubic feet**.
5	(a) 2048.717, 1700.05 (b) 3748.77	(a) 2048.7169 to 3dp = **2048.717**, 1700.054 to 2dp = **1700.05.** (b) 2048.717 + 1700.05 = 3748.767, which is **3748.77** to the nearest hundredth.
6	2,000,000	1 million = 1,000,000, 1 billion = 1,000,000,000, 1 trillion = 1,000,000,000,000. Therefore, 10 trillion ÷ 5 million = 10,000,000,000,000 ÷ 5,000,000 = **2,000,000**.
7	3471	17,846,529 to the nearest 10,000 is 17,850,000. Actual to rounded number difference is 17,846,529 – 17,850,000 = **3471**.
8	131	The 1st pattern has 7 circles and the common difference between patterns is 4. Number of circles for 32nd pattern = 7 for 1st pattern + (31 × 4) = 7 + 124 = **131**.
9	54	219 = 7 circles for 1st pattern + 4(n – 1) for adding 4 to each remaining pattern. 219 = 7 + 4(n – 1) where n is the pattern number required. 219 – 7 = 4(n – 1) → 212 = 4(n – 1) → 53 = n – 1 → 53 + 1 = n, therefore, n = **54**.
10	A = 1 B = 25	Odd-numbered terms are a sequence of square numbers. Even-numbered terms are a sequence of triangular numbers. Missing term A is the first triangular number which is **1**. Missing term B is the 5th square number which is **25**.
11	2.25, 1, –0.25, –1.5	Term 1 = 3.5 – 5(1) ÷ 4 = **2.25** Term 2 = 3.5 – 5(2) ÷ 4 = **1** Term 3 = 3.5 – 5(3) ÷ 4 = **–0.25** Term 4 = 3.5 – 5(4) ÷ 4 = **–1.5**
12	5n + 3	8 circles make up pattern 1; common difference of 5 between patterns. Using 5n + ? = 8 where n = 1 for pattern 1, 5(1) + ? = 8, ? = 3. Therefore, rule is **5n + 3**.
13	S	94 ÷ 7 = 13 remainder 3. This indicates 13 repeat patterns (13 × 7 = 91) and 3 squares into the 14th pattern. The third square into the pattern has an **S** on it.
14	25 – 5n	The first term is 20 and the common difference between adjacent terms is –5. Create 1st term answer of 20 by adjusting –5n i.e. ? – 5n = 20. When n = 1, ? – 5(1) = 20, therefore ? = 20 + 5, ? = 25. Rule is **25 – 5n**.
15	55.4, 50.9, 46.4, 41.9, 37.4, 32.9	To 1dp, 46.39 is 46.4, 50.88 is 50.9, 55.41 is 55.4, 41.92 is 41.9, 37.37 is 37.4, 32.86 is 32.9. Descending sequence is: **55.4, 50.9, 46.4, 41.9, 37.4, 32.9**.

Factors and Multiples - Beginner, page 10

Question	Answer	Explanation
1	6	Any whole number that divides exactly into a whole number N is termed a factor. This includes 1 and the number N itself. Factors of 12 are: 1, 2, 3, 4, 6, 12, a total of **6**.
2	7	The number **7** has only two factors, 1 and 7, which sum to 8.
3	18	Factors of 10 are: 1, 2, 5 and 10, the sum of which is 1 + 2 + 5 + 10 = **18**.
4	1, 3 and 9	Factors of 9 are: 1, 3, 9 Factors of 18 are: 1, 2, 3, 6, 9, 18 Common factors are **1, 3 and 9**.
5	28	Numbers less than 50 that are divisible by both 2 and 7 include, 14, 28 and 42. Only **28** has digits which equal 16 when multiplied.
6	5	Factors of 15 are: 1, 3, 5, 15 Factors of 20 are: 1, 2, 4, 5, 10, 20 The highest common factor (HCF) is **5**.
7	34	The 3rd multiple of 7 is 3 × 7 = 21. The 5th multiple of 11 is 5 × 11 = 55. 55 − 21 = **34**
8	9	First nine multiples of 9 are 18, 27, 36, 45, 54, 63, 72, 81 and 90. The missing multiple must be the first multiple which is **9**.
9	18	Multiples of 6 are: 6, 12, 18, 24, 30... Multiples of 9 are: 9, 18, 27, 36... The smallest number common to both is **18**.
10	630	As each pack contains 6 pens, the number of pens in each box = 15 × 6 = 90. The number of pens in 7 boxes is therefore equal to 7 × 90 = **630**.
11	10:25	Duration of 5 rides + 4 breaks = (5 × 7min) + (4 × 5min) = 35min + 20min = 55min. As the first ride starts at 09:30, the 5th ride will end 55min later at **10:25**.
12	45	Multiples of 9 are: 9, 18, 27, 36, 45, 54... Multiples of 15 are: 15, 30, 45, 60... The lowest common multiple (LCM) is **45**.
13	4 and 14	The numbers **4 and 14** are the only numbers from the list that are factors of 28 and multiples of 2.
14	5, 10 and 20	Factors of 20 are: 1, 2, 4, 5, 10, 20 Multiples of 5 are: 5, 10, 15, 20, 25... Numbers that are both factors of 20 and multiples of 5 are **5, 10 and 20**.
15	12	Factors of 24 are: 1, 2, 3, 4, 6, 8, 12, 24. The correct number is **12** as it is a factor of 24, a multiple of 3 and a number >7 and <22.

Factors and Multiples - Intermediate, page 11

Question	Answer	Explanation
1	1 and 78, 2 and 39, 3 and 26, 6 and 13	Factors of 78 are: 1, 2, 3, 6, 13, 26, 39 and 78. Factor pairs are: **1 and 78, 2 and 39, 3 and 26, 6 and 13**.
2	3657	A composite number is a whole number that can be divided evenly by numbers other than 1 or itself. From the list, the composite numbers are 415, 323, 117 and 2802. Sum of the composite numbers = 415 + 323 + 117 + 2802 = **3657**.
3	1, 2, 3, 6, 9	Factors of 36: 1, 2, 3, 4, 6, 9, 12, 18, 36. Factors of 54: 1, 2, 3, 6, 9, 18, 27, 54. Combination lock code is first 5 common factors which are **1, 2, 3, 6, 9**.
4	14	Factors of 28 are: 1, 2, 4, 7, 14, 28. Factors of 56 are: 1, 2, 4, 7, 8, 14, 28, 56. Factors of 70 are: 1, 2, 5, 7, 10, 14, 35, 70. HCF is **14**.
5	2, 3 and 5	Note that the factors of 30 are 1, 2, 3, 5, 6, 10, 15 and 30. Composite number is 15. Prime factors are **2, 3 and 5**.
6	24	The product of the prime factors from the factorisation process gives number N. Therefore, $N = 2 \times 2 \times 2 \times 3 =$ **24**.
7	A = 59 B = 413	As the common difference between adjacent terms is 59, the first eight multiples of 59 are therefore A, 118, 177, 236, 295, 354, B and 472. A = 118 − 59 = **59** (i.e. 1st multiple) and B = 354 + 59 = **413** (i.e. 7th multiple).
8	168	Multiples of 28 are 28, 56, 84, 112, 140, 168, 196... Multiples of 42 are 42, 84, 126, 168, 210... The second smallest common multiple is **168**.
9	75	As the 3rd multiple of N is 15, N must be 15 ÷ 3 = 5. Sum of the first five multiples = 5 + 10 + 15 + 20 + 25 = **75**.
10	(a) 4140 (b) 690	(a) The number of special offer eggs taken away by customers must be a number in the list divisible by 18 (i.e. 18 eggs). The only number is **4140**. (b) Number of sales of boxes = 4140 ÷ 6 = **690**.
11	4 and 13	The only whole numbers that have a multiple of 52 are 1, 2, 4, 13, 26 and 52. Of these, only **4 and 13** have a LCM of 52 and are both less than 20.
12	108	The LCM of 12, 18 and 27 is **108**.
13	126	The 7th multiple of 18 is 126. The HCF of 28 and 42 is 14. The LCM of 126 and 14 is **126**.
14	(a) 1 and 13 (b) 78	(a) Shaded area factors are the common factors of 26 and 39, i.e. **1 and 13**. (b) The LCM of the three highest factors (13, 26 and 39) is **78**.
15	(a) 220 (b) 12	(a) Multiples of 20 are: 20, 40, 60, 80, 100, 120, 140, 160, 180, 200, 220, 240... Multiples of 44 are: 44, 88, 132, 176, 220, 264... The number **220** is the LCM of 20 and 44 and its digits also sum to 4. (b) Factors of 220 are: 1, 2, 4, 5, 10, 11, 20, 22, 44, 55, 110, 220, a total of **12** factors.

Factors and Multiplies - Advanced, page 12

Question	Answer	Explanation
1	(a) 1, 2, 3, 4, 6 and 12 (b) 2 and 3	(a) Common factors of 48, 60 and 84 are: **1, 2, 3, 4, 6 and 12**. (b) Prime numbers of common factors are: **2 and 3**.
2	2 × 2 × 3 × 7	Factors of 84 are: 1, 2, 3, 4, 6, 7, 12, 14, 21, 28, 42, 84. Prime factors are 2, 3 and 7. 84 as a product of prime factors = **2 × 2 × 3 × 7**.
3	25	1, 5 and 25 satisfy the criteria (through trial and error). Composite number is therefore **25**.
4	A → 6, 12, B → 15, C → 10, 20, D → 3, E → 2, 4, F → 5, G → 1	Factors of 12 are 1, 2, 3, 4, 6, 12. Factors of 15 are 1, 3, 5, 15. Factors of 20 are 1, 2, 4, 5, 10, 20. Area factors are: **A → 6, 12, B → 15, C → 10, 20, D → 3, E → 2, 4, F → 5, G → 1**.
5	2, 5, 7 and 13	Factors of 910 are: 1, 2, 5, 7, 10, 13, 14, 26, 35, 65, 70, 91, 130, 182, 455, 910. Prime factors of 910 are: **2, 5, 7 and 13**.
6	342	HCF of 54 and 72 is 18. HCF of 76 and 95 is 19. Product of HCFs = 18 × 19 = **342**.
7	91	The 6th multiple of N = (364 + 728) ÷ 2 = 1092 ÷ 2 = 546. Therefore, $6N$ = 546 and N = 546 ÷ 6 = **91**.
8	(a) 12 days (b) 24 days	For John, multiples of 6 are: 6, 12, 18, 24, 30... For Saud, multiples of 8 are: 8, 16, 24, 32, 40... For Sam, multiples of 12 are: 12, 24, 36, 48, 60... (a) From the multiples above: in **12 days**, John and Sam play on the same day. (b) From the multiples above: in **24 days**, they all play on the same day.
9	129	The 9th multiple of 86 equals 9 × 86 = 774. Number required = 774 ÷ 6 = **129**.
10	$^2/_3$	At 2pm, crowd number = 9 × 76 = 684. At 4pm, crowd number = 8 × 57 = 456. Crowd number at 4pm relative to 2pm = 456 ÷ 684 = 38 ÷ 57 = $^2/_3$.
11	Cell A = 53 Cell B = 318	The numbers in the rows and columns of the table are based on consecutive multiples of 53. 1st multiple of 53 is 1 × 53, cell A = **53**, cell B = 265 + 53 = **318**.
12	1,386	The LCM of 22, 33 and 99 is 198. 7th multiple of 198 = 7 × 198 = **1,386**.
13	(a) 42 (b) 2, 3 and 7	Multiples common to 14 and 21 are 42, 84 and 126. Factors of 42 are: 1, <u>2</u>, <u>3</u>, 6, <u>7</u>, 14, 21, 42. Factors of 84 are :1, 2, 3, 4, 6, 7, 12, 14, 21, 28, 42, 84. Factors of 126 are: 1, 2, 3, 6, 7, 9, 14, 18, 21, 42, 63, 126. (a) The HCF of 42, 84 and 126 is **42**. (b) The prime factors of 42 are shown <u>underlined</u> above and are **2, 3 and 7**.
14	8	Factors of 39 are: 1, 3, 13, 39. Prime factors of 39 are 3 and 13. Sum of prime factors multiplied by 3 = (3 + 13) × 3 = 16 × 3 = 48. 6th multiple of N = 48. N = 48 ÷ 6 = **8**.
15	(a): 8 (b): 728 (c): 2, 7, 13 (d): 182	(a) The HCF of 32, 40 and 56 is **8**. (b) The 91st multiple of answer (a) is 8 × 91 = **728**. (c) The three different prime factors of answer (b) are **2, 7 and 13**. (d) The LCM of answer (c) is **182**.

Fractions and Decimals - Beginner, page 14

Question	Answer	Explanation
1	**120**	$\frac{3}{4}$ of 160 = $\frac{3}{4} \times 160 = 3 \times 40 =$ **120**.
2	**$\frac{4}{8} = \frac{1}{2}$**	The left diagram is mapped out in eighths, four of which are shaded. i.e. $\frac{4}{8}$. The right diagram is mapped out in halves, one of which is shaded. i.e. $\frac{1}{2}$. Therefore, $\frac{4}{8} = \frac{1}{2}$.
3	**$\frac{1}{4}$**	There are 12 letters in the word, 3 of which are 'A'. Fraction is $\frac{3}{12} = \frac{1}{4}$.
4	**$\frac{1}{12}$**	As there are 360° in a circle, the fraction is 30° ÷ 360° = **$\frac{1}{12}$**.
5	**$\frac{1}{6}$**	$\frac{1}{2} - \frac{1}{3} = \frac{3}{6} - \frac{2}{6} =$ **$\frac{1}{6}$**
6	**$\frac{1}{8}$**	$\frac{1}{2} \div 4 = \frac{1}{2} \div \frac{4}{1} = \frac{1}{2} \times \frac{1}{4} =$ **$\frac{1}{8}$**
7	**1.9m**	3.4m – 1.5m = **1.9m**
8	**£7**	As the number in the tenths column is a 4 and is <5, the amount is rounded down to **£7**.
9	**0.006**	The product of 0.3 and 0.02 = 0.3 × 0.02 = **0.006**.
10	**0.357**	As a decimal, 35.7% = 35.7 ÷ 100 = **0.357**.
11	**7.7l**	7.672 litres = 7,672ml. 7,672ml to the nearest 100ml is 7,700ml. 7,700ml = 7.7 litres i.e. **7.7l**.
12	**16**	3.2 + 3.2 + 3.2 + 3.2 + 3.2 = 16, and 16 ÷ 3.2 = 5. Therefore the common number is **16**.
13	**$5\frac{21}{50}$**	$5.42 = 5\frac{42}{100} =$ **$5\frac{21}{50}$**
14	**0.625**	The left diagram is mapped out in quarters, two of which are shaded: $\frac{2}{4} = \frac{1}{2}$ The right diagram is mapped out in sixteenths, two of which are shaded: $\frac{2}{16} = \frac{1}{8}$ Therefore, $\frac{1}{2} + \frac{1}{8} = \frac{4}{8} + \frac{1}{8} = \frac{5}{8} =$ **0.625**.
15	**$\frac{72}{5}$**	3.6 ÷ 0.25 = 360 ÷ 25 = **$\frac{72}{5}$**

Fractions and Decimals - Intermediate, page 15

Question	Answer	Explanation
1	$1/6, 1/4, 1/3, 3/8, 3/5, 5/6, 7/8$	Writing the fractions $3/8, 1/6, 3/5, 7/8, 1/4, 5/6, 1/3$ with a lowest common denominator of 120 gives: $45/120, 20/120, 72/120, 105/120, 30/120, 100/120, 40/120$. Therefore, fractions in ascending order of size are: $\mathbf{1/6, 1/4, 1/3, 3/8, 3/5, 5/6, 7/8}$.
2	**14**	Number of cakes unsold = $9 - 6\,2/3 = 2\,1/3$. Number of slices (sixths) unsold = $(2 \times 6) + (1/3 \times 6) = 12 + 2 = \mathbf{14}$.
3	$5/9$	Procedure: Sum the two fractions and divide result by 2 to find halfway value: Sum = $2/3 + 4/9 = 6/9 + 4/9 = 10/9$. Dividing by 2 gives: $10/9 \div 2 = \mathbf{5/9}$.
4	$3/4$ and $5/8$	The two fractions $3/4$ and $5/8$ sum to $1\,3/8$. $3/4 + 5/8 = 6/8 + 5/8 = 11/8 = 1\,3/8$
5	$8\,5/8$	$3\,5/6 \times 18/8 = 23/6 \times 9/4 = 69/8 = \mathbf{8\,5/8}$
6	**14**	$1/12 + 1/16 = 4/48 + 3/48 = 7/48$, $7/48 \times 96 = 7 \times 2 = \mathbf{14}$
7	**74,400ml**	As 1 litre = 1000ml, 74.352 litres = 74,352ml. As the number in the tens column is ≥5 i.e. 5, the number in the hundreds column is increased from 3 to 4 giving **74,400ml** to the nearest 100ml.
8	**£160.86**	£1126 ÷ 7 = £160.85714, which is **£160.86** to 2dp.
9	**1674.2**	Cancel down to leave 83.71 × 10 = 837.1. 837.1 ÷ 0.5 = 2 × 837.1 = **1674.2**.
10	**90cm**	Side A = (0.15 ÷ 0.01)cm = (15 ÷ 1)cm = 15cm. Side B = (2.4 × A)cm = 2.4 × 15cm = 36cm. Side C = (2.6 × A)cm = 2.6 × 15cm = 39cm. Perimeter = 15cm + 36cm + 39cm = **90cm**.
11	**0.808**	As $N + N + N + N + N = 6.9$, $5N = 6.9$, therefore, $N = 6.9 \div 5 = 1.38$. $N - 0.572 = 1.38 - 0.572 = \mathbf{0.808}$.
12	**£425.32**	16% of £430.50 = $16/100 \times$ £430.50 = £68.88. Sale cost of television = £430.50 − £68.88 = £361.62. Sale cost of DVD player = 0.65 × £98 = £63.70. Total cost = £361.62 + £63.70 = **£425.32**.
13	**11.5**	First, divide out the fractional part i.e. 5073 ÷ 10,000 = 0.5073. Mixed number as a decimal is now 11 + 0.5073 = 11.5073. 11.5073 to 1dp is **11.5**.
14	(a) 0.4375 (b) 21	(a) Fraction of blue + yellow balloons = $3/8 + 3/16 = 6/16 + 3/16 = 9/16$. Fraction that are red = $1 - 9/16 = 7/16$. $7/16$ as a decimal is **0.4375**. (b) As there are 48 balloons in the packet, number that are red = $7/16$ of 48. $7/16 \times 48 = 7 \times 3 = \mathbf{21}$
15	$266/25$	10.64 as a mixed number is $10\,64/100 = 10\,16/25 = \mathbf{266/25}$.

Fractions and Decimals - Advanced, page 16

Question	Answer	Explanation
1	$\frac{7}{8}$	$1\frac{5}{6} + F = 2\frac{17}{24} \rightarrow F = 2\frac{17}{24} - 1\frac{5}{6} = \frac{65}{24} - \frac{11}{6} = \frac{65}{24} - \frac{44}{24} = \frac{21}{24} = \frac{7}{8}$
2	$\frac{21}{20}$L	$\frac{3}{5} + \frac{1}{10} + \frac{7}{8} = \frac{24}{40} + \frac{4}{40} + \frac{35}{40} = \frac{63}{40}$ Quantity in 3 tanks = $\frac{63}{40} \times 2$L = $\frac{126}{40}$L. Quantity of water in each tank = $\frac{1}{3}$ of $\frac{126}{40}$L = $\frac{126}{120}$L = $\frac{21}{20}$L.
3	$3\frac{3}{32}$	$\frac{2}{3} + 1\frac{1}{6} = \frac{2}{3} + \frac{7}{6} = \frac{4}{6} + \frac{7}{6} = \frac{11}{6}$ $1\frac{7}{8} - \frac{3}{16} = \frac{15}{8} - \frac{3}{16} = \frac{30}{16} - \frac{3}{16} = \frac{27}{16}$ $\frac{11}{6} \times \frac{27}{16} = \frac{11}{2} \times \frac{9}{16} = \frac{99}{32} = 3\frac{3}{32}$
4	£96.20	$N = \frac{1}{2} \times 80 = 40$, Bag 1: $\frac{9}{5} \times 40 = 72$, Bag 3: $\frac{3}{8} \times 40 = 15$, Bag 4: $\frac{3}{10} \times 40 = 12$ Total money = (72 × £1) + (40 × 50p) + (15 × 20p) + (12 × 10p) = £72 + £20 + £3 + £1.20 = **£96.20.**
5	$1\frac{3}{4}$	Fractions in ascending order are: $\frac{11}{33}, \frac{10}{25}, \frac{5}{10}, \frac{10}{16}, \frac{12}{18}, \frac{14}{20}, \frac{9}{12}, \frac{21}{24}$ 3rd largest is $\frac{14}{20}$ and 2nd smallest is $\frac{10}{25}$. $\frac{14}{20} \div \frac{10}{25} = \frac{14}{20} \times \frac{25}{10} = \frac{7}{4} = 1\frac{3}{4}$
6	15	Jane's share of the 48 sweets = $\frac{7}{8} \times 48 = 7 \times 6 = 42$. John's initial share of sweets = $\frac{5}{6} \times 42 = 5 \times 7 = 35$. John eats $\frac{4}{7} \times 35 = 4 \times 5 = 20$, leaving John with 35 − 20 = **15.**
7	8222.917	98,675 ÷ 12 = 8222.916667. As the 4th number to the right of the point is a 6, i.e. ≥5, the 3rd number past the point increases by 1 to give **8222.917** to 3dp.
8	28.444	6.82 = 7 to nearest whole number, 12.51 = 12.5 to nearest tenth, 8.739 = 8.74 to nearest hundredth, 0.2042 = 0.204 to nearest thousandth. Sum of rounded numbers = 7 + 12.5 + 8.74 + 0.204 = **28.444.**
9	550g	35 × 0.0157kg = 0.5495kg. As there are 1000g in 1kg, 0.5495kg = 549.5g, which is 550g to the nearest gram.
10	64.9cm	Largest length of brick L = 21.5cm + 4mm = 215mm + 4mm = 219mm. Largest width of brick W = 10.25cm + 3mm = 102.5mm + 3mm = 105.5mm. Perimeter of brick top = (2 × 219mm) + (2 × 105.5mm) = 649mm = **64.9cm.**
11	(a) $2\frac{5}{6}$ (b) $\frac{17}{6}$ (c) 2.833	(a) Total area shaded = $2\frac{10}{12} = 2\frac{5}{6}$. (b) $2\frac{5}{6}$ as an improper fraction = ((2 × 6) + 5) ÷ 6 = $\frac{17}{6}$. (c) $\frac{17}{6}$ as a decimal = 17 ÷ 6 = 2.8333... = **2.833** to 3dp.
12	7.71	As $7\frac{3}{4} - 2\frac{3}{8} = P$, $P = \frac{31}{4} - \frac{19}{8} = \frac{62}{8} - \frac{19}{8} = \frac{43}{8}$ or $5\frac{3}{8}$. $\frac{7}{8} \div \frac{3}{8} = \frac{7}{8} \times \frac{8}{3} = \frac{7}{3}$ or $2\frac{1}{3}$. Therefore, $(\frac{7}{8} \div \frac{3}{8}) + P = 2\frac{1}{3} + 5\frac{3}{8} = 7\frac{17}{24}$. $7\frac{17}{24} = 7.708333...$ which is **7.71** to the nearest hundredth.
13	17.28cm²	Box length L = 12cm. Box width W = $\frac{2}{5}$ of L = $\frac{2}{5} \times 12 = 4.8$cm. Box height H = $\frac{3}{10}$ of L = $\frac{3}{10} \times 12 = 3.6$cm. Smallest area = W × H = 4.8 × 3.6 = **17.28cm².**
14	207.36cm³	Volume V = end area × L = 17.28 × 12 = **207.36cm³**.
15	13.813	T = 4.25. T² = 4.25 × 4.25 = 18.0625. T² − T = 18.0625 − 4.25 = 13.8125 = **13.813** to 3dp.

Percentages, Ratios and Proportions - Beginner, page 18

Question	Answer	Explanation
1	4	5% of 80 = $(5/100) \times 80 = 0.05 \times 80$ = **4**.
2	36	Number of tins sold is 10% of 40 = $(10/100) \times 40 = 0.1 \times 40 = 4$. Number of unsold tins of paint = 40 − 4 = **36**.
3	29%	Percentage of white counters = 100% − (23% + 48%) = 100% − 71% = **29%**.
4	£13.50	50% of £9 = £9 ÷ 2 = £4.50. Mel has saved £9 + £4.50 = **£13.50**.
5	9	If 40% are to be shaded black then 60% (100% − 40%), will remain unshaded. Number of unshaded stars = 60% of 15 = $(60/100) \times 15 = 0.6 \times 15$ = **9**.
6	4:3	Divide each part of the ratio by the highest common factor (HCF) to reduce the ratio to its lowest terms. As the HCF of 12 and 9 is 3, the ratio 12:9 is **4:3** in its lowest terms.
7	2:3	Number of children = 80 − number of adults (32) = 48. Ratio of adults to children is therefore 32:48. 32:48 is **2:3** in its simplest form.
8	21	The 14 in the first ratio is 7 times the 2 in the second ratio. The missing number must therefore be 7 times the 3 in the second ratio. Therefore, ? = 7 × 3 = **21**.
9	25	5:4 is equivalent to ?:20. Note that the common multiple is 5 as 5 × 4 = 20. ? = 5 × 5 = 25. Therefore, there are **25** red beads in the necklace.
10	36	4:3 is equivalent to ?:27. Note that the common multiple is 9 as 9 × 3 = 27. ? = 9 × 4 = 36. Therefore, there are **36** triangles with a smiley face.
11	1/3	A proportion is a quantity that is part of a whole. Observe from the pattern that 2 of the 6 squares are shaded. The proportion of shaded squares is therefore $2/6$ reducing to **$1/3$**.
12	20%	Proportion of children is $9/45$ which reduces to $1/5$. $(1/5) \times 100$ = **20%**
13	50	As 3 out of the 5 circles in the pattern are shaded, the number of repeated patterns required to reach 30 shaded circles = 30 ÷ 3 = 10. Total number of circles = 10 × 5 = **50**.
14	8cm	1:5 is equivalent to ?:40. Note that the common multiple is 8 as 8 × 5km = 40km. ? = 8 × 1cm = 8cm. Therefore, the distance between towns on the map is **8cm**.
15	30m	1:600 is equivalent to 5:?. Note that the common multiple is 5 as 5 × 1cm = 5cm. ? = 5 × 600cm = 3,000cm. Therefore, the real length of the garden is **30m**.

Percentages, Ratios and Proportions - Intermediate, page 19

Question	Answer	Explanation
1	**6%**	Percentage means 'out of 100'. To convert a decimal or a fraction into a percentage multiply by 100. Therefore, 0.06 × 100 = **6%**.
2	**96%**	Percentage of apples that go bad = $(3/75) \times 100$ = 4%. Percentage of apples fit to eat = 100% − 4% = **96%**.
3	**16kg**	The 12kg represents 100% − 25% = 75% of a full bag (F). $(75/100) \times F = 12kg \rightarrow 0.75 \times F = 12kg \rightarrow F = 12kg \div 0.75 =$ **16kg**.
4	**44**	Percentage of counters left in the box = 100% − 45% = 55%. Number of counters left in the box = $(55/100) \times 80 =$ **44**.
5	**40%**	0.2 × 100 = 20% and $(2/5) \times 100$ = 40%. Percentage of boxes unsold at the end of Day 2 = 100% − (20% + 40%) = **40%**.
6	**18%**	Number of children on the bus = 50 − 41 = 9. Percentage of children on the bus = $(9/50) \times 100 = 9 \times 2 =$ **18%**.
7	**3:2**	Ratio of flats to houses is 72:48. Dividing each part of the ratio by 24 gives the ratio in its lowest terms, i.e. **3:2**.
8	**12**	Dividing the total number of circles by the sum of the ratio parts gives: 21 ÷ (4 + 3) = 21 ÷ 7 = 3. Number of circles to be shaded = 3 × 4 = **12**.
9	**26 days**	Dividing the total number of days in June by the sum of the ratio parts gives: 30 ÷ (13 + 2) = 30 ÷ 15 = 2. Number of dry days = 2 × 13 = **26 days**.
10	**24 red cars** **84 blue cars**	Dividing the total number of cars by the sum of the ratio parts gives: 108 ÷ (2 + 7) = 108 ÷ 9 = 12. Number of red cars = 12 × 2 = **24**. Number of blue cars = 12 × 7 = **84**.
11	**$2/5$**	The repeating pattern of the first five hexagons contains two shaded hexagons. Proportion of shaded hexagons is therefore **$2/5$**.
12	**78**	Number of cold drinks sold = 35% of 120 = $(35/100) \times 120 = 7 \times 6 = 42$. Number of hot drinks sold = 120 − 42 = **78**.
13	**48**	Number of repeated patterns = total number of tiles with a cross ÷ number of tiles with a cross in the given pattern: 36 ÷ 3 = 12. Number of tiles with a dot in 12 repeated patterns = 12 × 4 = **48**.
14	**20m^2**	As 1cm = 0.5m, actual room length (L) = 10 × 0.5 = 5m. Actual room width (W) = 8 × 0.5 = 4m. Area of room = L × W = 5m × 4m = **20m^2**.
15	**4cm**	400m = 40,000cm. As the scale is 1:10,000, 1cm on the map represents 10,000cm in reality. Therefore, the distance between roundabouts on the map = 40,000cm ÷ 10,000 = **4cm**.

Percentages, Ratios and Proportions - Advanced, page 20

Question	Answer	Explanation
1	(a) $^{131}/_{200}$ (b) 0.655	(a) $65.5\% = {}^{65.5}/_{100} = {}^{655}/_{1000} = \mathbf{{}^{131}/_{200}}$ (b) $65.5\% = {}^{655}/_{1000} = \mathbf{0.655}$
2	M = 15,360 F = 18,960 C = 13,680	Number of adult males M = 32% of 48,000 = $({}^{32}/_{100}) \times 48,000 = 32 \times 480 = \mathbf{15,360}$. Number of adult females F = $({}^{395}/_{1000}) \times 48,000 = 395 \times 48 = \mathbf{18,960}$. Number of children C = 48,000 − (15,360 + 18,960) = 48,000 − 34,320 = **13,680**.
3	85.92%	£11,895 − £1,675 = £10,220 £10,220 as a % of £11,895 = $({}^{10,220}/_{11,895}) \times 100 = 85.91845... = \mathbf{85.92\%}$ to 2dp.
4	23.5	$N + (20\% \text{ of } 62.5) = (85\% \text{ of } 60) − 15 \rightarrow N + (({}^{20}/_{100}) \times 62.5) = (({}^{85}/_{100}) \times 60) − 15$ $\rightarrow N + (0.2 \times 62.5) = (8.5 \times 6) − 15 \rightarrow N + 12.5 = 51 − 15 \rightarrow N = 36 − 12.5 = \mathbf{23.5}$.
5	1,203,546,400	1.5% of 1,185,760,000 = $({}^{1.5}/_{100}) \times 1,185,760,000 = 17,786,400$. Population after 1 year = 1,185,760,000 + 17,786,400 = **1,203,546,400**.
6	5:7:8:13	Divide ratio parts by the highest common factor, i.e. 7 in this case. $^{35}/_7 : {}^{49}/_7 : {}^{56}/_7 : {}^{91}/_7$. Therefore, ratio is **5:7:8:13**.
7	17:11:6	Number of blue beads = 272 − (136 + 88) = 272 − 224 = 48. Yellow to green to blue bead ratio = 136:88:48 which reduces to **17:11:6**.
8	185	Tea sales = 75. Teas sold ÷ ratio part = $^{75}/_{15}$ = 5. Coffee sales = 5 × 11 = 55, Hot chocolate sales = 5 × 7 = 35, Bottled water sales = 5 × 4 = 20. Total drink sales = 75 + 55 + 35 + 20 = **185**.
9	5:7:9	From table, thin sliced loaves = 25, med. sliced = 1.4 × 25 = 35, thick sliced = 25 + 80% of 25 = 25 + $(({}^{80}/_{100}) \times 25)$ = 25 + 20 = 45. Ratio of thin to medium to thick loaves = 25:35:45 which reduces to **5:7:9**.
10	£7.68	£25.60 = 2,560p. 2,560p ÷ (1 + 2 + 5 + 8) = 2,560p ÷ 16 = 160p. Wayne receives 8 × 160p = 1,280p. 1,280p ÷ (2 + 3) = 1,280 ÷ 5 = 256p. Pari gets 3 × 256p = 768p or **£7.68**.
11	(a) 15 (b) 96min	(a) In 1min, number of cars entering car park = 18 ÷ 6 = 3. Number entering in 5min = 3 × 5 = **15**. (b) Time taken in minutes for 288 cars to enter car park = 288 ÷ 3 = **96min**.
12	(a) 8min (b) 60 miles	(a) Time taken to complete 4 miles = $^4/_6$ of 12min = **8min**. (b) 7200s ÷ 60 = 120min. As the car travels 4 miles in 8min, in 120min, car travels $({}^{120}/_8) \times 4$ miles = **60 miles**.
13	(a) $^5/_{12}$ (b) 4:5	(a) Number of yellow circles = $^1/_3$ of 12 circles = 12 ÷ 3 = 4. As ratio of yellow to red circles is 4:3, number of red circles must be 3. Number of blue circles = 12 − (4 + 3) = 5. Proportion of blue circles = $\mathbf{{}^5/_{12}}$. (b) Ratio of yellow to blue circles is **4:5**.
14	161mm	Width of Atlantic on map in cm = 4,830 ÷ 300 = 16.1cm. Width of Atlantic on map in mm = 16.1 × 10 = **161mm**.
15	(a) 3.5m (b) 3m^2	(a) As scale is 1:50, 1cm on map is 50cm in reality. Therefore, L1 = 2 × 50 = 100cm or 1m. L2 = $^{L1}/_2$ = $^{100cm}/_2$ = 50cm or 0.5m. L3 = 2L1 = 2 × 100cm = 200cm or 2m. Length L = L1 + L2 + L3 = 1m + 0.5m + 2m = **3.5m**. (b) As L4 = L1 = 1m, area of picture P1 = L1 × L4 = 1m × 1m = 1m^2. Area of picture P2 = L3 × L4 = 2m × 1m = 2m^2. Area of both pictures = 1m^2 + 2m^2 = **3m^2**.

Algebra and Number Machines - Beginner, page 22

Question	Answer	Explanation
1	2	$x \div 2 = 1$. Multiply both sides by 2. Therefore, $x = 2 \times 1 = \mathbf{2}$.
2	16	$h - 5 = 11$. Add 5 to both sides. Therefore, $h = 11 + 5 = \mathbf{16}$.
3	10x - 22	Multiply 2 by 5x = 10x. Middle sign is -. Multiply 2 by 11 = 22. Therefore, $\mathbf{10x - 22}$.
4	40	Substitute in $z = 7$ and $y = 1$. Therefore, $8(7 - (2 \times 1)) = 8 \times (7 - 2) = 8 \times 5 = \mathbf{40}$.
5	$ab/2$	Area of triangle = $1/2 \times$ base $\times$ height. Therefore, the expression is $1/2 \times a \times b = \mathbf{ab/2}$.
6	4	$x \times x \times x = x^3 = 64$. Cube root both sides. Therefore, $x = \sqrt[3]{64} = \mathbf{4}$.
7	12x	The membership fee for one month is x. Therefore, the membership fee for 12 months is $x \times 12 = 12x$
8	9000	$9x = 9 \times x$. Substitute in $x = 1000$. Therefore, $9 \times 1000 = \mathbf{9000}$.
9	3	$24 - 6c = 2c$. Add 6c to both sides. $24 = 2c + 6c = 8c$. Divide both sides by 8. Therefore, $c = 24 \div 8 = \mathbf{3}$.
10	59	$y = 6x + 23$. Substitute in $x = 6$. Therefore, $y = (6 \times 6) + 23 = 36 + 23 = \mathbf{59}$.
11	4	Working forwards from the input, $(15 + 1) \div 4 = 16 \div 4 = \mathbf{4}$.
12	−99	Working forwards from the input, $-9 \times 11 = \mathbf{-99}$.
13	17	Working backwards from the output, $(46 - 12) \div 2 = 34 \div 2 = \mathbf{17}$.
14	1.8	Working forwards from the input, $(149 \times 0) + 1.8 = 0 + 1.8 = \mathbf{1.8}$.
15	53	Working forwards from the input, $106 - (106 \div 2) = 106 - 53 = \mathbf{53}$.

Algebra and Number Machines - Intermediate, page 23

Question	Answer	Explanation
1	13	$(x + 7) \div 8 = 2.5$. Multiply both sides by 8. $x + 7 = 8 \times 2.5 = 20$. Subtract 7 from both sides. Therefore, $x = 20 - 7 = $ **13**.
2	28	The car is $3 + (100 \div 4) = 3 + 25 = $ **28** years old.
3	14	$-6y + 64 = -20$. Subtract 64 from both sides. $-6y = -20 - 64 = -84$. Divide both sides by -6. Therefore, $y = -84 \div -6 = $ **14**.
4	−27	Substitute in $p = -0.75$ and $q = 4$. $2 \times -0.75 \times ((3 \times 4) - (8 \times -0.75)) = -1.5(12 - -6) = -1.5(12 + 6) = -1.5 \times 18 = $ **−27**
5	$6x - 1$	Perimeter of the kite: $2x + 2(2x - 0.5) = 2x + 4x - 1 = $ **$6x - 1$**.
6	4	$22b - 11.2 = 108.8 - 8b$. Add $8b$ to both sides. $22b + 8b - 11.2 = 30b - 11.2 = 108.8$. Add 11.2 to both sides. $30b = 108.8 + 11.2 = 120$. Divide both sides by 30. Therefore, $b = 120 \div 30 = $ **4**.
7	$-14x(4x + 1)$	Highest common factor is -14. Also, x is common in both terms. $-14x \times 4x - 14x \times (1)$ **$-14x(4x + 1)$**
8	54cm	Perimeter of triangle: $x + (x + y) + (x - y) = x + x + x + y - y = 3x$. Substitute in $x = 18$cm. Therefore, the perimeter of the triangle is 3×18cm = **54cm**.
9	62p	Total cost of 6 unshaded pentagons at 55p each: 6×55p = 330p/£3.30 Total cost of 10 shaded pentagons is unknown. So say it is x. £3.30 + 10x = £9.50. 10x = £9.50 - £3.30. Therefore 10x = £6.20 Therefore x = £6.20 $\div$ 10 = **62p**.
10	4	Substitute in $x = 2$. $5w = 6(10 - 3(2)) - w = 6(10 - 6) - w = 6(4) - w = 24 - w$. $5w = 24 - w$. Add w to both sides. Therefore, $5w + w = 6w = 24$. Divide both sides by 6. Therefore, $w = 24 \div 6 = $ **4**.
11	15	Working forwards from the input, $(224 \div 7) - 17 = 32 - 17 = $ **15**.
12	100	Working forwards from the input, $(^1/_2 + ^1/_6) \times 150 = (^3/_6 + ^1/_6) \times 150$. Therefore, $^4/_6 \times 150 = {}^{600}/_6 = $ **100**.
13	113	Working backwards from the output, $((65 \times 8) + 45) \div 5 = (520 + 45) \div 5$. Therefore, $565 \div 5 = $ **113**.
14	315	Working forwards from the input, $(5 + 2^4) \times \sqrt{225} = (5 + 16) \times 15 = 21 \times 15 = $ **315**.
15	4.7	Output = Input 2 − Input 1 = 13.35 − 8.7 = 4.65. The number 5 (second decimal place) is ≥ 5, so the number 6 (first decimal place) is rounded up to 7 to give an output of **4.7** to one decimal place.

Algebra and Number Machines - Advanced, page 24

Question	Answer	Explanation
1	**24cm**	Perimeter of shape is $8x + 1.1x + 2.7x + 4.6x + 2.6x + 4.6x + 2.7x + 1.1x = 27.4x$. Therefore, the perimeter is $27.4x = 657.6$cm. Divide both sides by 27.4. Therefore, $x = 657.6$cm $\div 27.4 =$ **24cm**.
2	**83.58**	Substitute in $a = -0.45$, $b = 0.95$ and $c = 0.5$. Therefore, $z = 6(-(-0.45) + 10 \times 0.95)(2 \times 0.95 - 0.5)$. $z = 6(0.45 + 9.5)(1.9 - 0.5) = 6 \times 9.95 \times 1.4 =$ **83.58**.
3	**$5n + 4$**	$(8 \times (n + 1) + 2n) \div 2 = (8n + 8 + 2n) \div 2 = (10n + 8) \div 2 =$ **$5n + 4$**
4	**2**	$56x + 143 = 42 + 109x - 5$ simplifies to $56x + 143 = 37 + 109x$. Subtract $56x$ from both sides. $143 = 37 + 109x - 56x \rightarrow 143 = 37 + 53x$ Subtract 37 from both sides. $143 - 37 = 106 = 53x$. Divide both sides by 53. Therefore, $x = 106 \div 53 =$ **2**.
5	**£495.90**	Amount daughter received: $x \times \frac{1}{4} =$ £275.50. $x =$ £275.50 $\div \frac{1}{4} =$ £275.50 $\times \frac{4}{1} =$ £275.50 $\times 4 =$ £1102. Amount son received: £1102 $\times 15\% =$ £1102 $\times 0.15 =$ £165.30. Amount spent on music equipment: £1102 $-$ (£275.50 $+$ £165.30) $=$ £661.20. Therefore, the difference is £661.20 $-$ £165.30 $=$ **£495.90**.
6	**2.5**	$((215 + 6^3) \times ?) - 25 = ((215 + 216) \times ?) - 25 = (431 \times ?) - 25 = 1052.5$. $431 \times ? = 1052.5 + 25 = 1077.5$. Therefore, the missing number is $1077.5 \div 431 =$ **2.5**.
7	**3.97**	$(24 \times 34) - (2095 \div 5) = 816 - 419 = 397 = 100P$ Therefore, $P = 397 \div 100 =$ **3.97**.
8	**486.5**	$2780 + 2780 + 2780 + 1390 = 9730 = ? \times 20$ Therefore, the missing number is $9730 \div 20 =$ **486.5**.
9	**87.2**	Working backwards from the output: $((535 - 219) \times 0.2) + 24 = (316 \times 0.2) + 24 = 63.2 + 24 =$ **87.2**.
10	**$6x^2$**	To calculate the area of the shape, split it into three rectangles. Area of the shape: $(2x \times x) + (2x \times x) + (2x \times x) = 2x^2 + 2x^2 + 2x^2 =$ **$6x^2$**
11	**−20**	$x^3 \div 2 = -4000$. Therefore, $x^3 = -4000 \times 2 = -8000$. Cube root both sides. $x = \sqrt[3]{-8000} =$ **−20**.
12	**37.07**	Working forwards from the input, $((-1.38 + 8.62) \times 6.5) - 9.99$ $= (7.24 \times 6.5) - 9.99 = 47.06 - 9.99 =$ **37.07**.
13	**$2(2r + s)$**	Perimeter of the shape: $(4 \times r) + s + t + (s - t) = 4r + 2s + t - t = 4r + 2s$ $=$ **$2(2r + s)$**
14	**$\frac{55}{18}$**	$\frac{3y}{5} - 2\frac{1}{3} = \frac{3y}{5} - \frac{7}{3} = -\frac{1}{2}$. Add $\frac{7}{3}$ to both sides. $\frac{3y}{5} = -\frac{1}{2} + \frac{7}{3} = -\frac{3}{6} + \frac{14}{6} = \frac{11}{6}$ Therefore, $y = \frac{11}{6} \div \frac{3}{5} = \frac{11}{6} \times \frac{5}{3} =$ **$\frac{55}{18}$**.
15	**XXXII**	Working forwards from the input, $((CXXV + L) \div V) - III = ((125 + 50) \div 5) - 3$ $= (175 \div 5) - 3 = 35 - 3 = 32 =$ **XXXII**.

Averages and Representing Data - Beginner, page 26

Question	Answer	Explanation
1	12	Range: highest value – lowest value Therefore, the highest value = range + lowest value = 8 + 4 = **12**.
2	3	Sum of numbers: 0 + 1 + 2 + 3 + 4 + 5 + 6 = 21. Therefore, the mean is 21 ÷ 7 = **3**.
3	20	Sum of numbers: 19 + 14 + 11 + 31 + 7 + 27 + 31 = 140. Therefore, the mean is 140 ÷ 7 = **20**.
4	19	Counters in ascending order: 7, 11, 14, 19, 27, 31, 31. There are 7 values in total. 7 is an odd number so the median (middle) number is the fourth value. Therefore, the median is **19**.
5	31	The mode is **31** as it is the most frequently occurring number (2 times).
6	24	Range: highest value – lowest value Therefore, the range is 31 – 7 = **24**.
7	9	The modal shoe size is **9** as it is the most frequently occurring size (5 people).
8	6°C	Sum of temperatures: 6°C + 5°C + 3°C + 9°C + 7°C = 30°C. Therefore, the average temperature is 30°C ÷ 5 = **6°C**.
9	65	The pie chart shows that half are Birch trees. Therefore, the number of Birch trees is 130 ÷ 2 = **65**.
10	70 mph	Average speed (miles/h) = distance travelled (miles) ÷ time (h). 35 miles ÷ 30min = 35 miles ÷ 0.5h = **70 mph**
11	42	Number of pens given away: 20 + 8 + 10 + 4 = **42.**
12	16	Number of houses with a garden: 9 + 5 + 2 = **16**.
13	30%	Number of pupils who liked both sports: 9. Total number of pupils: 11 + 9 + 7 + 3 = 30. Therefore, the percentage is $^9/_{30} \times 100 = ^3/_{10} \times 100$ = **30%**.
14	4	The number of computers sold each week were as follows: week 1 (750), week 2 (500), week 3 (1250), week 4 (1250), week 5 (375), week 6 (500), week 7 (1500). **4** of the 7 weeks saw ≤ 900 computers sold.
15	18	Number of people owning at least one phone: 9 + 6 + 3 = **18**.

Averages and Representing Data - Intermediate, page 27

Question	Answer	Explanation
1	$^{109}/_{90}$	Sum of fractions: $^{4}/_{3} + ^{2}/_{3} + ^{5}/_{3} + ^{3}/_{2} + ^{8}/_{9} = ^{24}/_{18} + ^{12}/_{18} + ^{30}/_{18} + ^{27}/_{18} + ^{16}/_{18} = ^{109}/_{18}$. Therefore, the average is $^{109}/_{18} \div 5 = ^{109}/_{(18 \times 5)} = \mathbf{^{109}/_{90}}$.
2	6.05g	Weights in ascending order: 5.0g, 5.4g, 5.8g, 6.3g, 6.5g, 6.9g There are 6 values in total. 6 is an even number so the median number is the mean of the third and fourth values (middle values). Therefore, the median is (5.8g + 6.3g) ÷ 2 = 12.1g ÷ 2 = **6.05g**.
3	3.4cm	1.7cm + 3.5cm + 1.7cm + 7.7cm + 1.7cm + 4.0cm + 3.5cm = 23.8cm Therefore, the mean is 23.8cm ÷ 7 = **3.4cm**.
4	35mm	Lengths in ascending order: 1.7cm, 1.7cm, 1.7cm, 3.5cm, 3.5cm, 4.0cm, 7.7cm There are 7 values in total. 7 is an odd number so the median number is the fourth value. Therefore, the median is 3.5cm = **35mm**.
5	1.7cm	The mode is **1.7cm** as it is the most frequently occurring number (three times).
6	60mm	Range: highest value – lowest value Therefore, the range is 7.7cm – 1.7cm = 6cm = **60mm**.
7	20%	Season 1: (10 × 3 points) + (4 × 1 point) = 30 points + 4 points = 34 points. Calculating the number of points in seasons 2 to 5 in the same way gives: season 2 (30 points), season 3 (35 points), season 4 (36 points) and season 5 (31 points). Therefore, the percentage of seasons with >35 points: $^{1}/_{5} \times 100 = \mathbf{20\%}$.
8	21	The pie chart shows that $^{1}/_{8}$ said music was their favourite subject. Therefore, the number who said music was their favourite is 168 ÷ 8 = **21**.
9	33	Total number of people with a 50p, £2 coin or both: 8 + 11 + 7 + 1 + 6 = **33**.
10	25°C	Temperatures in ascending order: 22°C, 24°C, 25°C, 25°C, 26°C, 26.5°C, 27°C There are 7 values in total. 7 is an odd number so the median number is the 4th value. Therefore, the median is 25°C. The mode is 25°C as it is the most frequently occurring number (2 times). Therefore, the average of the median and mode = (25°C + 25°C) ÷ 2 = **25°C**.
11	37°C	26°C – (–11°C) = 26°C + 11°C = **37°C**
12	25.1°C	(26.5°C + 27°C + 24°C + 22°C + 26°C) ÷ 5 = 125.5°C ÷ 5 = **25.1°C**
13	27km/h	The trains meet 40 minutes into the journey for train S and 20 minutes into the journey for train F. Speed of train S = 18km ÷ 40min = 18km ÷ $^{2}/_{3}$hr = 27km/h. Speed of train F = 18km ÷ 20min = 18km ÷ $^{1}/_{3}$hr = 54km/h. Therefore, difference in speeds = 54km/h – 27km/h = **27km/h**.
14	7	Mean score history: (20 + 35 + 40 + 25 + 30) ÷ 5 = 150 ÷ 5 = 30. Mean score science: (30 + 25 + 15 + 20 + 25) ÷ 5 = 115 ÷ 5 = 23. Difference in scores for subjects = 30 – 23 = **7**.
15	26.5 pints	Reading across at 15l, the approximate conversion is **26.5 pints**.

Averages and Representing Data - Advanced, page 28

Question	Answer	Explanation
1	16.2	Smallest number = $\frac{3}{4} \times 18 = 13.5$. The dataset in ascending order consists of 13.5, 18, 18, 18 and an unknown value. The median value is halfway through the sorted dataset, which is 18. The largest value is $1.65 \times 18 = 29.7$. Range = largest value − smallest value = $29.7 − 13.5 =$ **16.2**.
2	$\frac{13}{175}$	Total number of people having all 3 carpet colours: $52 − 40 = 12$. Total number of people: $78 + 40 + 89 + 32 + 12 + 26 + 73 = 350$. Number of people having green and blue but not red: 26. The fraction of people having green and blue but not red is $\frac{26}{350} = \frac{13}{175}$.
3	£600	Mean: $(28°C + 34°C + 30°C + 16°C + 28°C + 26°C) \div 6 = 162°C \div 6 = 27°C$. Temperatures in ascending order: 16°C, 26°C, 28°C, 28°C, 30°C, 34°C. Median: 28°C. Overall spent: $(2 \times £150) + (2 \times £100) + (2 \times £50) =$ **£600**.
4	£6.60	Price per hat: $£2.40 \div 8 = £0.30$. Price per balloon: $£0.30 \div 3 = £0.10$. Total price of balloons: $£0.10 \times 12 = £1.20$. Total price of plates: $£0.15 \times 20 = £3.00$. Total: $£2.40 + £1.20 + £3.00 =$ **£6.60**.
5	22	Smallest number = 9; largest number = $9 + 26 = 35$. Sum of the four numbers = 88. Therefore, the sum of the two unknown values = $88 − (9 + 35) = 88 − 44 = 44$. The mode, which occurs twice, must be $44 \div 2 =$ **22**.
6	3.74	Sum of ratio parts: $1 + 2 + 2 + 3 = 8$. Smallest value: $\frac{1}{8} \times 14.96 = 1.87$. Largest value: $\frac{3}{8} \times 14.96 = 5.61$. Therefore, the range is $5.61 − 1.87 =$ **3.74**.
7	382.5	Cricket balls used each year: year 1 ($5 \times 120 = 600$), year 2 ($2.5 \times 120 = 300$), year 3 ($3.25 \times 120 = 390$) and year 4 ($2 \times 120 = 240$). Mean number of cricket balls used per year: $(600 + 300 + 390 + 240) \div 4 =$ **382.5**.
8	Monday	$3^4 − \sqrt{144} − 4^3 = 81 − 12 − 64 = 5$ $5°C + 5°C = 10°C \rightarrow$ **Monday**
9	5	$(10 + 9 + 2 + 7 + 1 + 1) \div 6 = 30 \div 6 =$ **5**
10	3.5	Scores in ascending order: 1, 1, 1, 2, 3, 3, 4, 5, 7, 8, 9, 10 There are 12 values in total. 12 is an even number so the median score is the mean of the sixth and seventh values (middle values). Therefore, the median is $(3 + 4) \div 2 =$ **3.5**.
11	4.5	$(3 + 4 + 1 + 8 + 5 + 3 + 10 + 9 + 2 + 7 + 1 + 1) \div 12 = 54 \div 12 =$ **4.5**
12	8	Range: $10 − 1 = 9$. Mode: 1. Range − mode = $9 − 1 =$ **8**.
13	$\frac{7}{12}$	Number of students: 12 Number of students who scored < 5: 7 Fraction of students who scored < 5: $\frac{7}{12}$
14	CML	Values in ascending order: 18, 20, 25, 32, 46, 59. There are 6 values in total. 6 is an even number so the median is the mean of the 3rd and 4th values (middle values). Therefore, the median is $(25 + 32) \div 2 = 28.5$. Mean: $(18 + 20 + 25 + 32 + 46 + 59) \div 6 = 200 \div 6 = 33\frac{1}{3}$. Median × mean = $28.5 \times 33\frac{1}{3} = 950 =$ **CML** in Roman numerals.
15	5p	Number of coins: $(1 \times 6) + (3 \times 5) + (2 \times 2) + (5 \times 4) = 45$. Value of each coin: $£2.25 \div 45 = £0.05 =$ **5p**.

Measures and Reading Scales - Beginner, page 30

Question	Answer	Explanation
1	**11cm**	10mm = 1cm → 110mm ÷ 10 = **11cm**
2	**11,400g**	1kg = 1000g → 11.4kg × 1000 = **11,400g**
3	**800ml**	1L = 1000ml → 0.8l × 1000 = **800ml**
4	**100,000g**	Combined weight of objects = 34kg + 35kg + 31kg = 100kg. 1kg = 1000g → 100kg × 1000 = **100,000g**
5	**5 miles**	1760 yards = 1 mile → 8800 yards ÷ 1760 = **5 miles**
6	**5.5L**	1 pint ≈ 0.5L → 11 pints × 0.5 = **5.5L**
7	**36L**	Reading on petrol gauge = (32L + 40L) ÷ 2 = 72L ÷ 2 = **36L**.
8	**2.3kg**	The scale goes up in divisions of 0.1kg. The arrow is at the third division after 2.0kg, which is equal to **2.3kg**.
9	**25°C**	The scale goes up in divisions of 1°C. The thermometer shows a temperature of five divisions above 20°C, which is equal to 20°C + 5°C = **25°C**.
10	**70mm**	The scale goes up in divisions of 2cm. The arrow points halfway between 6cm and 8cm, which is equal to 7cm. As 1cm = 10mm, 7cm × 10 = **70mm**.
11	**4cm**	As the scale is 1:225, 9m is drawn with a height of 9m ÷ 225 = 900cm ÷ 225 = **4cm**.
12	**400kg**	The scale goes up in divisions of 0.2 tonnes. The arrow is at the third division after 2.0 tonnes, which is equal to 2.6 tonnes. 3 tonnes − 2.6 tonnes = 0.4 tonnes 1 tonne = 1000kg → 0.4 tonnes × 1000 = **400kg**
13	**2.1cm**	2.4cm − 0.3cm = **2.1cm**
14	**10**	Volume of water in container: 1.5L = 1500ml Number of 150ml glasses of water required: 1500ml ÷ 150ml = **10**.
15	**1km**	As the scale is 1:50,000, 2cm on the map represents a distance of 2cm × 50,000 = 100,000cm = 1000m = **1km**.

Measures and Reading Scales - Intermediate, page 31

Question	Answer	Explanation
1	2,350g	150,000mg ÷ 1,000 = 150g 0.0025 tonnes × 1,000 = 2.5kg, 2.5kg × 1,000 = 2,500g. Therefore, the difference is 2,500g − 150g = **2,350g**.
2	10.5mm	49.5mm = 4mm + 6mm + 2mm + 6mm + 5mm + 9mm + 3mm + $x$mm + 4mm Therefore, 49.5mm = (39mm + $x$mm) → x = 49.5mm − 39mm = **10.5mm**.
3	13.75 gallons	1 gallon ≈ 4l = 4,000ml Therefore, 55,000ml ≈ 55,000ml ÷ 4,000 = **13.75 gallons**.
4	140cm	Carol's height = 80% × 1.75m = $\frac{4}{5}$ × 1.75m = 1.4m = **140cm**.
5	100 ounces	1 pound = 16 ounces → 18.75 pounds × 16 = 300 ounces Therefore, the weight of one printer = 300 ounces ÷ 3 = **100 ounces**.
6	£162	$226.8 ÷ $1.4 = 162 £1 × 162 = **£162**
7	2050ml	The scale on the jug goes up in main divisions of 0.4L. Amount of water in jug: 1.2L + 0.2L = 1.4L = 1400ml. Amount of water in container: 650ml + 1400ml = **2050ml**.
8	−13.75°C	The scale goes up in divisions of 5°C. Average temperature: (−20°C + (−7.5°C)) ÷ 2 = −27.5°C ÷ 2 = **−13.75°C**.
9	£4.48	Weight of butter: 1.4kg Cost per 250g: 80p → Cost per kg = 4 × 80p = 320p. 320p × 1.4 = 448p = **£4.48**.
10	8cm	280m = 28,000cm 28,000cm ÷ 3500 = **8cm**
11	133 $\frac{1}{3}$mm²	Width of rectangle = 2.4cm − 0.4cm = 2cm = 20mm. Height of rectangle = 20mm ÷ 3 = 6 $\frac{2}{3}$mm. Area of rectangle = 20mm × 6 $\frac{2}{3}$mm = **133 $\frac{1}{3}$mm²**.
12	225g	The scale goes up in divisions of 0.25kg. Total weight of objects: 1.625kg = 1625g. Weight of rice box = 1625g − (5 × 280g) = 1625g − 1400g = **225g**.
13	0.275m	5 feet 9 inches = (5 × 12 inches) + 9 inches = 60 inches + 9 inches = 69 inches. 1 inch ≈ 2.5cm → 69 inches × 2.5 ≈ 172.5cm = 1.725m Therefore, 2m − 1.725m = **0.275m**.
14	0.02m	Nail A: 2.4cm; Nail B: 4.6cm. Therefore, the difference in length: 4.6cm − 2.4cm = 2.2cm = 0.022m = **0.02m** to (2dp).
15	6.16m	2.8cm × 220 = 616cm = **6.16m**

Measures and Reading Scales - Advanced, page 32

Question	Answer	Explanation
1	3.6	Amount of water in container: 2.25L = 2250ml. Amount of additional water needed to fill container: 2700ml − 2250ml = 450ml. 1 pint ≈ 500ml → 1/4 pint = 500 ÷ 4 = 125 ml. 450ml ÷ 500 = 0.9 pints. Number of quarter pint glasses required to fill 0.9 pints: 0.9 ÷ 0.25 = **3.6.**
2	70,400 yards/h	Time interval: 1800 seconds (30 minutes) to 3600 seconds (60 minutes). Distance travelled: 20 miles = 20 × 1760 yards = 35,200 yards. Time taken for journey: 60min − 30min = 30min = 0.5hr. Speed = distance travelled ÷ time taken = 35,200 yards ÷ 0.5hr = **70,400 yards/h.**
3	0.85L	Amount of water in container at start: 3L × 3/4 = 2.25l = 2250ml. 80ml of water is lost every minute, so in 17.5 minutes, 1400ml (80 × 17.5) will be lost. Therefore, the amount of water left is 2250ml − 1400ml = 850ml = **0.85l**.
4	774,400m²	√256mm = 16mm 16mm × 55,000 = 880,000mm = 880m 880m × 880m = **774,400m²**
5	9.447kg	Left side of scales: $^{20}/_8$kg + 5kg + 392g = 7.892kg. Right side of scales: 9.7kg + 7kg + 639g = 17.339kg. 17.339kg − 7.892kg = **9.447kg**
6	671.4 inches	1,000mm (1m) ≈ 3 feet → 18.65m × 3 = 55.95 feet 1 foot = 12 inches → 55.95 feet × 12 = **671.4 inches**
7	32,680 ounces	0.817 tonnes = 817,000g 1 ounce ≈ 25g → 817,000g ÷ 25 = **32,680 ounces**
8	7744 ounces	Weight of 8 crates: 12 stone 8 pounds = (12 × 14) pounds + 8 pounds = 168 pounds + 8 pounds = 176 pounds = 16 ounces × 176 = 2816 ounces. Weight of 1 crate: 2816 ounces ÷ 8 = 352 ounces. Therefore, the weight of 22 crates is 352 ounces × 22 = **7744 ounces**.
9	£0.65	50p × 4 = 200p = £2.00 and £1.20 × 7 = £8.40 0.5L × 4 = 2L and 2L × 7 = 14L 2L + 14L = 16L £2.00 + £8.40 = £10.40 £10.40 ÷ 16 = **£0.65**
10	0.7 tonnes	A:B:C:D = 1:1:1:7 Sum of ratio parts: 1 + 1 + 1 + 7 = 10. The reading on the scales is 1000kg. 1000kg ÷ 10 = 100kg 100kg × 7 = 700kg = **0.7 tonnes**
11	490.53cm	17.101cm + 470.8cm + 2 $^5/_8$cm = 490.526cm = **490.53cm** to 2 decimal places
12	11.5°C	Temperatures in ascending order: −46°C, 9°C, 14°C, 14.75°C Median temperature: (9°C + 14°C) ÷ 2 = **11.5°C.**
13	XX	Length of straight line: 2mm. Length of one side of pentagon: 8mm. Perimeter of regular pentagon: 8mm × 5 = 40mm. Number of straight lines needed to build pentagon = 40mm ÷ 2mm = 20. This is **XX** in Roman numerals.
14	120	2 $^2/_5$m = 240cm. 20mm = 2cm. 240cm ÷ 2cm = **120** coins
15	0.33m³	Length = 5.5cm = 0.055m. Width = 2.5cm = 0.025m. Height = 3cm = 0.03m. Actual dimensions: L: 0.055m × 20 = 1.1m; B: 0.025m × 20 = 0.5m; H: 0.03m × 20 = 0.6m. Volume of cuboid in reality = 1.1m × 0.5m × 0.6m = **0.33m³**.

Dates, Time and Timetables - Beginner, page 34

Question	Answer	Explanation
1	31 days	There are **31 days** in the month of January.
2	Sunday	If 25th November is a Monday, the previous Monday would have been the 18th, the Monday before that would have been the 11th, so the 10th would be the day before that Monday which would have been a **Sunday**.
3	6 days	He has **6 days**: 18th, 19th, 20th, 21st, 22nd, 23rd.
4	13th July	The date will be a week from Friday the 6th. 6th + 7 days → 13th Therefore, the date is **13th July**.
5	4	The next Friday would be the 5th of October, then the 12th, then the 19th, and then the 26th. Therefore, there will be **4** visits to the gym in October.
6	6hr	There are **6 hours** between 10.00am and 4.00pm.
7	8min	1 minute = 60 seconds 480sec ÷ 60sec = **8min**
8	4.30pm	The hour hand is halfway between 4 and 5 and the minute hand is on 6. 6 × 5min = 30min Therefore, the time shown is **4.30pm**.
9	9.55pm	9.10pm + 45 minutes = **9.55pm**
10	00:30	The first hour after midnight is the first hour in the day. Half an hour is equal to 30 minutes. Therefore, the 24-hour time is **00:30**.
11	19:19	7.19pm is the nineteenth hour in the day. Therefore, the 24-hour time is **19:19**.
12	98min	06:25 to 07:25 → 1hr = 60min 07:25 to 08:03 → 38min 60min + 38min = **98min**
13	14:45	Looking at Boat A, the difference between 10:00 and 11:30 is 90 minutes. Therefore, Boat B will arrive at Windsor 90 minutes after 13:15 → **14:45**.
14	Woking	6.40pm is 18:40 in 24-hour clock format. The flat tyre occurs 45 minutes after 18:40 → 19:25. The next stop for the bus after 19:25 would have been **Woking** at 19:28.
15	7.50am	The journey duration is 7.25am to 8.15am → 50min. Point B is 50% into the journey. 50% of 50min = 0.5 × 50min = 25min. Therefore, she passes point B at 7.25am + 25min = **7.50am**.

© 2017 ElevenPlusExams.co.uk — COPYING STRICTLY PROHIBITED

Dates, Times and Timetables - Intermediate, page 35

Question	Answer	Explanation
1	91 days	Number of days in: April + May + June = 30 + 31 + 30 = **91 days**
2	$^5/_7$	Number of days in February: 28, Saturdays: 6th, 13th, 20th, 27th, Sundays: 7th, 14th, 21st, 28th. Therefore, there are 8 weekend days in total. Therefore, the fraction of days that are weekdays is $^{(28-8)}/_{28} = ^{20}/_{28} = ^5/_7$.
3	Wednesday	Days in October: Monday 5th – 4 days → Thursday 1st October Days in September: Wednesday 30th – 30 days → Tuesday 1st September Days in August: Monday 31st – 6 days → **Wednesday** 26th August
4	Yousef	Mary was born in 2006 (MMVI), Jai in 2011 (MMXI), Yousef in 1900 (MCM), Peter in 1950 (MCML) and June in 2000 (MM). Therefore, **Yousef** was born first.
5	1,461 days	In any four year period there will be one leap year and three non leap years. Therefore, the total number of days = 366 days + (3 × 365 days) = 366 days + 1095 days = **1461 days**.
6	5 days	Clock A is 2.5 minutes faster than clock B → 2.5 × 60sec = 150sec. Therefore, it will take clock A, 150 ÷ 30 = **5 days** to read the same as clock B.
7	135min	13:34 (1.34pm) to 3.49pm → 2hr 15min = 60min + 60min + 15min = **135min**
8	14:25	Time in London: 11.25pm – 9hr → 2.25pm = **14:25**.
9	64hr	1 day = 24 hours $2\,^2/_3$ × 24hr = **64hr**
10	85min	Left clock: 5.15am Right clock: 6.40am The number of minutes between both times is 45min + 40min = **85min**.
11	7.10am	60min × $^1/_6$ = 10min 10min before 7.20am is **7.10am**.
12	21:53	Journey time for train X is 10:34 to 12:08 → 94min Journey time for train Y is 20:07 + 94min + 720sec (12min) → 20:07 + 106min = **21:53**.
13	Bishopthorpe	The journey duration is 15:31 to 16:07 → 36min. 60% into the journey is 60% of 36min = 0.6 × 36min = 21.6min. 21.6min after 15:31 is 15:52 and 36sec, the last stop was **Bishopthorpe** (15:45).
14	5min	Journey times: Bus A (09:30 to 10:23) → 53min, Bus B (09:45 to 10:38) → 53min, Bus C (10:00 to 10:58) → 58min. The range of times = 58min – 53min = **5min**.
15	146min	Time train should have left Gateshead: 09:16 + 5min = 09:21. Time train should have arrived in Peterborough: 11:53 – 6min = 11:47. Therefore, journey time should have been: 09:21 to 11:47 → **146min**.

Dates, Time and Timetables - Advanced, page 36

Question	Answer	Explanation
1	30 $\frac{1}{3}$ days	Number of days in the 9 months between January and September: 31 + 28 + 31 + 30 + 31 + 30 + 31 + 31 + 30 = 273 days. Therefore, the average number of days per month = 273 ÷ 9 = **30 $\frac{1}{3}$ days**.
2	4,212min	00:07 on Sunday is 47hr 53min before 00:00 on Tuesday. 22:19 is 22hr 19min after 00:00 on Tuesday. Therefore, the length between the times is 47hr 53min + 22hr 19min = 70hr 12min = (60 × 70 + 12)min = **4,212min**.
3	10.02am	The time on the clock is 10.10am. The first time in the table is 10.02am, which is 8 minutes short of 10.10am. The second time is 13:20, which is 1.20pm and is further away from 10.10am than 10.02am. The third time is 10.30am, which is 20 minutes after 10.10am. The fourth time is 11.45am and the fifth time is around 11.03am and neither of these are closer to 10.10am than 10.02am. Therefore, the closest time to 10.10am is **10.02am**.
4	3.35pm	20min + 1.1hr + 1.1hr + 900sec + 1.2hr + 1.2hr + 40min + 1.15hr = (20 + 66 + 66 + 15 + 72 + 72 + 40 + 69)min = 420min = 7hr 7hr after 8.35am is **3.35pm**.
5	Tuesday	Tommy started on Tuesday 15th January. Workout the dates every seven days, the 22nd January, 29th January, 5th February, 12th February, 19th February, 26th February and 4th March are all Tuesdays. Remember that it is a leap year and February contains 29 days. Therefore, 4th March is a **Tuesday**.
6	186min	Journey times: train 1 (202min), train 2 (178min), train 3 (186min), train 4 (181min) and train 5 (186min). The times (minutes) in ascending numerical order are 178, 181, 186, 186 and 202. The median is **186min**.
7	270sec	4 $\frac{3}{5}$ hr = 4.6hr = 4.6 × 60min = 276min. 280.5min − 276min = 4.5min = 4.5 × 60sec = **270sec**
8	25%	Year 5 classes: 55 × 9 = 495 minutes, Year 4 classes: 45 × 6 = 270 minutes Total teaching time: 495 minutes + 270 minutes = 765 minutes As there are 60 minutes in an hour, she works 51 hours × 60 = 3060 minutes. To find teaching time as a percentage of total hours worked: $\frac{765}{3060}$ × 100 = $\frac{76500}{3060}$ = **25%**
9	402 days	Time studying: (50% × 366 days) + (60% × 365 days) = 183 days + 219 days = **402 days**.
10	2.27am	Time on clock face: 2.35am. Working forwards from the input, 2.35am + 360sec = 2.41am. 2.41am − 30min = 2.11am. 2.11am + 16min = **2.27am**.
11	6 weeks	Number of minutes in a week = 60 × 24 × 7 = 10,080min. Number of weeks in 60,480min is 60,480 ÷ 10,080 = **6 weeks**.
12	162hr	Length of journey: 15:02 to 15:38 → 36min. Amount of time travelling in year: 36min × 270 = 9720min = **162hr.**
13	20%	Five months contain less than 31 days: February, April, June, September and November. Of these, only one has more than eight characters in its name (September), which as a percentage is $\frac{1}{5}$ × 100 = **20%**.
14	Friday 8th at 6.00am	A week is seven days or 7 × 24 = 168hr. $\frac{3}{4}$ through this is 168hr × $\frac{3}{4}$ = 126hr = 5 days 6hr. Five days 6hr after 00:00 on Sunday 3rd is **Friday 8th at 6.00am**.
15	1460sec	Journey times: Jo (25min), Amy (30min), Brian (18min). Average journey time: (25 + 30 + 18)min ÷ 3 = 73min ÷ 3 = 24 $\frac{1}{3}$ min = **1460sec**.

Lines, Angles and Bearings - Beginner, page 38

Question	Answer	Explanation
1	**Q**	**Q** is a horizontal line.
2	**2.3cm**	Line A is parallel to line D and has a length of **2.3cm**.
3	**no**	**No** an oblique line cannot be parallel or perpendicular to the horizontal x-axis. Oblique lines are slanting lines.
4	**360°**	The interior angles of any quadrilateral add up to **360°**.
5	**140°**	Angles around a point add up to 360°. $k = 360° - 220° = $ **140°**.
6	**acute**	Angles less than 90° are called **acute** angles.
7	**75°**	An isosceles triangle has two equal angles. Angles in a triangle add up to 180°. $j + j + 30° = 180°$. Hence, $2j = 180° - 30° = 150°$. Therefore, $j = 150° \div 2 = $ **75°**.
8	**119°**	Angles in a quadrilateral add up to 360°. $q = 360° - (103° + 86° + 52°) = 360° - 241° = $ **119°**.
9	**20°**	Angles in a right angle add up to 90°. $p = 90° - (15° + 55°) = 90° - 70° = $ **20°**
10	**93°**	An obtuse angle is greater than 90° but less than 180°. The only obtuse angle in the list is **93°**.
11	**120°**	The interior angles in a hexagon sum to 720°. $m = 720° \div 6 = $ **120°**.
12	**east**	On a compass, **east** is directly opposite west.
13	**2**	On a compass, 180° (180° ÷ 90° = **2** right angles) are between north and south.
14	**A**	The house is southwest of the train station in diagram **A**.
15	**I**	Point **I** is east of point M.

Lines, Angles and Bearings - Intermediate, page 39

Question	Answer	Explanation
1	1.87m	$1870 \, ^3/_5$mm = 1870.6mm = 187.06cm = 1.8706m = **1.87m** to two decimal places.
2	5.1cm	The lengths of the lines that are perpendicular to line A in ascending numerical order are 1.376cm, 3.7cm, 5.1cm, 6cm, 8.2cm. The median (or middle) length of these five lengths is the third length, which is **5.1cm**.
3	3.68cm	Length of longest diagonal: 1.8cm + 7.4cm = 9.2cm. Length of shortest diagonal: 40% × 9.2cm = $^{40}/_{100}$ × 9.2cm = **3.68cm**.
4	577.21°	The interior angles in a hexagon add up to 720°. Sum of other angles = 720° − 142.79° = **577.21°**.
5	225°	$^5/_6$ × (3 × 90°) = $^5/_6$ × 270° = **225°**
6	240°	Angles in a circle add up to 360°. Each section of the circle is 360° ÷ 12 = 30°. The circle must be turned clockwise through eight sections so the arrow points to point P. Therefore, the wheel must be turned through 8 × 30° = **240°**.
7	67°	The trapezium has two pairs of equal angles. Therefore, x + x + 113° + 113° = $2x$ + 226° = 360°. $2x$ = 360° − 226° = 134° x = 134° ÷ 2 = **67°**
8	108.5°	An isosceles triangle has two equal angles, call them x. Angles in a triangle add up to 180°. x + x + 37° = 180°. Therefore, $2x$ = 180° − 37° = 143°. Therefore, x = 143° ÷ 2 = 71.5°. Angles on a straight line add up to 180°. a = 180° − 71.5° = **108.5°**.
9	52.5°	Angles in a right angle add up to 90°. t = 90° − 20° = 70°. u = 90° − 55° = 35°. Average size of angles t and u = (70° + 35°) ÷ 2 = 105° ÷ 2 = **52.5°**.
10	10.00am	If the hour hand turns through 150°, which is $^{150}/_{360}$ = $^5/_{12}$ of a clock turn, anticlockwise from 3.00pm, the new time will be $^5/_{12}$ × 12 hr = 5 hr back from 3.00pm → **10.00am**.
11	144°	Angles around the point at the centre of the pentagon add up to 360°. b = $^2/_5$ × 360° = **144°**.
12	225°	The clockwise turn from northeast to west on a compass is 45° + 180° = **225°**.
13	northeast	495° anticlockwise from south is **northeast**.
14	northwest	The number equivalent to Roman numerals LI on the grid is 51, which is **northwest** of the grey square.
15	southwest	Sophie is at the leisure centre, the post box is south of her and the library is southeast of her. Therefore, the hospital is **southwest** of Sophie.

Lines, Angles and Bearings - Advanced, page 40

Question	Answer	Explanation
1	56.775°	Angles in a triangle add up to 180°. Final angle = 180° − ($37\,^5/_8$° + $85\,^3/_5$°) = 180° − (37.625° + 85.6°) = 180° − 123.225° = **56.775°**
2	46.059	4 of the lines are perpendicular to side 1. Therefore, 4^3 − 17.941 = 64 − 17.941 = **46.059**.
3	37.5°	As the angle between any two adjacent numbers on a clock face is 30°. Therefore Angle A = 5 × 30° = 150°. A quarter of angle A is 150° ÷ 4 = **37.5°**.
4	165°	Sum of ratio parts: 3 + 4 + 11 + 6 = 24. As angles in a quadrilateral add up to 360°, each part is worth 360° ÷ 24 = 15°. Therefore, the largest angle is 11 × 15° = **165°**.
5	68.1°	Angles on a straight line add up to 180°. n = 180° − (43.8° + m). As $m = n$, n = 180° − (43.8° + n). n = 180° − 43.8° − n. $n + n$ = 136.2°. $2n$ = 136.2°. Therefore, n = 136.2° ÷ 2 = **68.1°**.
6	24°	Angles in a circle add up to 360°. 360° = (90° + 90° + k + 6.5k). 360° = 180° + 7.5k. 7.5k = 360° − 180° = 180°. Therefore, k = 180° ÷ 7.5 = **24°**.
7	361.96°	Obtuse angles are greater than 90° but less than 180°. Therefore, the sum of the obtuse angles in the list is 101.19° + 170.04° + 90.73° = **361.96°**.
8	62.2°	Angles on a straight line add up to 180°. s = 180° − 68.4° = 111.6°. Angles in a triangle add up to 180°. t = 180° − (19° + 111.6°) = 180° − 130.6° = 49.4°. Therefore, $s − t$ = 111.6° − 49.4° = **62.2°**.
9	234°	Interior angles of a pentagon add up to 540°. Therefore, $q + 2q + 2.5q + 3q + 6.5q = 15q$ = 540°. Hence, q = 540° ÷ 15 = 36°. Therefore, the largest angle = 6.5 × 36° = **234°**.
10	67.5°	Interior angles of an octagon add up to 1080°. As this is a regular octagon, each angle is 1080° ÷ 8 = 135°. x = 135° ÷ 2 = **67.5°**.
11	B	Imagine walking from the start square: **forward 3, turn left 90°, forward 2, turn right 90°, forward 3, turn left 90°, forward 7**.
12	29.2°	Angles on a straight line add up to 180°. Largest angle = 180° − 61.7° = 118.3°. The angle on the bottom right in the triangle = 180° − 147.5° = 32.5°. Angles in a triangle add up to 180°. y = 180° − (118.3° + 32.5°) = **29.2°**.
13	256.5°	2.85 × 90° = **256.5°**
14	southeast	Zoha is east of Jason and Kerstin is west of Arden. Zoha is at point 5, Jason at point 3, Kerstin at point 4 and Ardan at point 1. Amit is south of Ardan at point 2. Therefore, Amit is **southeast** of the school.
15	198.63°	3972.5° ÷ 20 = 198.625° = **198.63°** to two decimal places

2D Shapes, Perimeters, Areas and Symmetry - Beginner, page 42

Question	Answer	Explanation
1	trapezium	The shape is called a **trapezium**.
2	scalene	A triangle in which all sides are of different lengths is called a **scalene** triangle.
3	4	A regular octagon has **4** pairs of parallel sides.
4	7cm	Opposite sides of a parallelogram are equal in length. Therefore, the length of Y is **7cm**.
5	32cm	The diameter of a circle is double the length of the radius. Therefore, the diameter is 16cm × 2 = **32cm**.
6	1	A kite has two pairs of sides that are of the same length. Therefore, any side selected at random will leave **1** other side the same length.
7	heptagon	A 7-sided shape is called a **heptagon**.
8	200m^2	Area of oblong: 25m × 8m = **200m^2**.
9	121mm^2	Side length: 44mm ÷ 4 = 11mm. Therefore, the area is 11mm × 11mm = **121mm^2**.
10	10cm	Perimeter of rectangle: (2 × 8cm) + (2 × 3cm) = 16cm + 6cm = 22cm. Perimeter of triangle: 3cm + 4cm + 5cm = 12cm. Therefore, the difference is 22cm – 12cm = **10cm**.
11	100mm^2	Number of squares in rectangle R1: 6. Area of R1 is 6 × 10mm^2 = 60mm^2. Number of squares in rectangle R2: 4. Area of R2 is 4 × 10mm^2 = 40mm^2. Combined area of R1 and R2 is 60mm^2 + 40mm^2 = **100mm^2**.
12	17.5cm^2	Area of triangle: $^1/_2$ × base × perpendicular height $^1/_2$ × 5cm × 7cm = **17.5cm^2**
13	3	An equilateral triangle has **3** lines of symmetry.
14	2	The rhombus has an order of rotational symmetry of **2**. When rotated about its centre 360° it can map onto itself twice.
15	1	Shape **1** is shown with an incorrect line of symmetry.

© 2017 ElevenPlusExams.co.uk — COPYING STRICTLY PROHIBITED

2D Shapes, Perimeters, Areas and Symmetry - Intermediate, page 43

Question	Answer	Explanation
1	20	The square has 4 sides, the kite 4 sides, the pentagon 5 sides, the triangle 3 sides and the trapezium 4 sides. The total number of sides of the 5 shapes is 4 + 4 + 5 + 3 + 4 = **20**.
2	isosceles triangle	The shape is an **isosceles triangle**.
3	decagon	The more sides a polygon has the more it looks like a circle. The polygon with the most sides in the list is a **decagon**.
4	5.5cm	Radius of one circle = 330mm ÷ 6 = 55mm = **5.5cm.**
5	$^2/_5$	A polygon is a shape with three or more straight sides. Therefore, four of the five shapes are polygons. Of the five shapes, the rectangle and rhombus are the only shapes with at least one pair of parallel sides. As a fraction, this is $^2/_5$.
6	184	A regular quadrilateral is a shape with 4 equal straight sides and 4 equal angles. Therefore, 46 identical, regular quadrilaterals will have 4 × 46 = **184** sides which are equal in length.
7	nonagon	Sum of the interior angles of any polygon = $(n - 2) \times 180°$ where n = number of sides. Rearranging $(n - 2) \times 180° = 1260°$, gives n as 9. Therefore, the polygon is a **nonagon**.
8	3773cm	Side length: 2156cm ÷ 4 = 539cm. Therefore, the perimeter is 7 × 539cm = **3773cm**.
9	84.5cm^2	Side length of square: √169cm^2 = 13cm, which is also the base and perpendicular height of the triangle. Therefore, the area of the triangle is $^1/_2$ × 13cm × 13cm = **84.5cm^2**.
10	$a(a - b)$ or $a^2 - ab$	The area of the rectangle is $a \times (a - b) = a(a - b)$ or $a^2 - ab$
11	15.37m	3.90m + 4.96m + 1.95m + 4.56m = **15.37m**
12	180cm^2	The number of full squares contained within the shape is 18. The number of half squares contained within the shape is 4, which makes 2 further full squares. Therefore, the shape covers 18 + 2 = 20 full squares in total. As the area of one square is 9cm^2, the area of 20 squares is 9cm^2 × 20 = **180cm^2**.
13	2	**2** of the 7 letters (A and C) have at least one line of symmetry through their centre.
14	6	The full shape is a regular hexagon, which has **6** lines of symmetry in total.
15	2.8	The shapes below are listed with their order of rotational symmetry in brackets: equilateral triangle (3), square (4), parallelogram (2) and a rectangle (2). The average order of rotational symmetry of 2 equilateral triangles, 1 square, 1 parallelogram and 1 rectangle is the sum of the order of rotational symmetry of all 5 shapes divided by the number of shapes, which is (3 + 3 + 4 + 2 + 2) ÷ 5 = 14 ÷ 5 = **2.8**.

2D Shapes, Perimeters, Areas and Symmetry - Advanced, page 44

Question	Answer	Explanation
1	11.1m	Average side length = sum of side lengths ÷ number of sides = (? + 4m + 5m + 4m + 4m + 3m + 6m + 3m + 4m) ÷ 9 = 4.9m. (? + 33m) ÷ 9 = 4.9m → ? = (4.9m × 9) − 33m = 44.1m − 33m = **11.1m**.
2	$7.4x - 6.4$	The perimeter is given by the expression $(2 \times 1.4x) + (2 \times (2.3x − 3.2)) = 2.8x + 4.6x − 6.4$ = **$7.4x - 6.4$**.
3	25.2cm^2	Area of parallelogram = area of two triangles plus area of central square = ($^1/_2$ × 1.8cm × 4.2cm) + (4.2cm × 4.2cm) + ($^1/_2$ × 1.8cm × 4.2cm) = 3.78cm^2 + 17.64cm^2 + 3.78cm^2 = **25.2cm^2**.
4	50%	Of the 8 letters, 4 letters (C, M, E and W) have line symmetry but not rotational symmetry, which as a percentage is $^4/_8$ × 100 = **50%**.
5	LXm	Perimeter of shape: XVm + IIIm + Vm + XIIm + Vm + XIIm + Vm + IIIm = 15m + 3m + 5m + 12m + 5m + 12m + 5m + 3m = 60m = **LXm**.
6	36cm	Diameter of one circle = 1.5cm × 2 = 3cm. Side length of rhombus = 3 × diameter of one circle = 3 × 3cm = 9cm. Perimeter of rhombus = 4 × 9cm = **36cm**.
7	50.13cm	Area of triangle: $^1/_2$ × base × perpendicular height Therefore, the height is 1002.5cm^2 ÷ (40cm × $^1/_2$) = 1002.5cm^2 ÷ 20cm = 50.125cm = **50.13cm** to two decimal places.
8	10	The number of pairs of parallel sides of the shapes (from left to right) are 4 + 3 + 1 + 0 + 2 + 0 = **10**.
9	200cm^2	Area of rectangle R1 = 20cm × 3cm = 60cm^2. Area of rectangle R2 = (20cm − 14cm) × (20cm − 6cm) = 6cm × 14cm = 84cm^2. Area of rectangle R3 = 20cm × 3cm = 60cm^2. Therefore, the area of the whole shape is 60cm^2 + 84cm^2 + 60cm^2 = 204cm^2. 204cm^2 rounded to the nearest 10cm^2 is **200cm^2**.
10	1.7cm	Side length of each square: √1369mm^2 = 37mm = 3.7cm. Therefore, 3.7cm + x + 3.7cm + x + 3.7cm = 14.5cm → $2x$ + 11.1cm = 14.5cm. Therefore, $2x$ = 14.5cm − 11.1cm → x = 3.4cm ÷ 2 = **1.7cm**.
11	12,696.1	(8,083 × 1.6) − 236.7 = **12,696.1**
12	105,280cm	Diameter of circle is 0.0056km = 5.6m = 560cm = square side length. Perimeter of square = 4 × 560cm = 2240cm. Perimeters of 47 identical squares = 47 × 2,240cm = **105,280cm**.
13	28.4m^2	Area of rectangle = 4m × 7.1m = 28.4m^2. Area of triangle = $^1/_2$ × 8m × 7.8m = 31.2m^2. Area of square = 3.9m × 3.9m = 15.21m^2. The areas in ascending numerical order are 15.21m^2, 28.4m^2 and 31.2m^2. The median is **28.4m^2**.
14	27cm	Side length of square: 36cm ÷ 4 = 9cm. Area of square: 9cm × 9cm = 81cm^2. Area of rectangle = 4 × area of square = 4 × 81cm^2 = 324cm^2. Length of rectangle = area ÷ height = 324cm^2 ÷ 12cm = **27cm**.
15	A	Statement **A** is false as 100% of the shapes are polygons.

3D Shapes and Volumes - Beginner, page 46

Question	Answer	Explanation
1	**tetrahedron** or **triangular-based pyramid**	This 3D shape is called a **tetrahedron**, which is also known as a **triangular-based pyramid**.
2	**5**	A triangular prism has **5** faces.
3	**cone**	This 3D shape is called a **cone**.
4	**12**	A cube has **12** edges.
5	**10**	A pentagonal prism has **10** vertices.
6	**square-based pyramid**	When folded up, the net forms a **square-based pyramid**.
7	**2.5cm**	The height of the cuboid is **2.5cm**, the length is 6cm and the width is 2cm.
8	**cylinder**	When folded up, the net forms a **cylinder**.
9	**108m³**	9m × 4m × 3m = **108m³**
10	**4cm**	$\sqrt[3]{64cm^3}$ = **4cm**
11	**500cm³**	Volume of one cube: 100cm³ Therefore, the volume of 5 cubes = 5 × 100cm³ = **500cm³**.
12	**2cm³**	Number of cubes: 5 × 3 × 3 = 45. Therefore, the volume of one cube is 90cm³ ÷ 45 = **2cm³**.
13	**100cm³**	10cm × 2cm × 5cm = **100cm³**
14	**A**	Volume of cuboid A: 4cm × 9cm × 4cm = 144cm³. Volume of cuboid B: 5cm × 12cm × 2cm = 120cm³. Cuboid **A** has the larger volume.
15	**80m³**	Volume of cube B: 60m³ × ⅓ = 20m³. Therefore, the combined volume is 60m³ + 20m³ = **80m³**.

3D Shapes and Volumes - Intermediate, page 47

Question	Answer	Explanation
1	4	A hexagonal prism has **4** pairs of parallel faces.
2	2	A tetrahedron has 4 vertices and an octahedron has 6 vertices. Therefore, the difference is 6 − 4 = **2**.
3	35	The cube has 12 edges, the square-based pyramid 8 edges and the pentagonal prism 15 edges. Therefore, the total number of edges is 12 + 8 + 15 = **35**.
4	**triangular prism** or **square-based pyramid**	An octagonal prism has 10 faces. The shape with half the number of faces (which is $\frac{1}{2} \times 10 = 5$) is a **triangular prism** or **square-based pyramid**.
5	48	Number of spheres in box 1: $\frac{2}{3} \times 36 = 24$. Therefore, the number of hemispheres in box 1: 24 × 2 = **48**. 2 hemispheres = 1 sphere
6	130m	134,673mm = 13,467.3cm = 134.673m. The number 4 (units column) is < 5, so the 3 (tens column) remains a 3 to give **130m** to the nearest 10m.
7	87	A cube consists of 6 square faces. Elaine requires 24 × 6 = 144 squares in total. Therefore, she needs a further 144 − 57 = **87** squares.
8	E	Face **E** is parallel to the base of the cube when it is folded up.
9	1,320cm³	11cm × 6cm × 0.2m = 11cm × 6cm × 20cm = **1,320cm³**
10	49m²	If the volume of a cube is 343m³, the side length must be $(\sqrt[3]{343})$m = 7m. Therefore, the area of one square face is 7m × 7m = **49m²**.
11	162cm³	Volume of wedge = $\frac{1}{2}$ × length × height × width $\frac{1}{2}$ × 9cm × 6cm × 6cm = **162cm³**
12	3m	Volume of cuboid = length × height × width Therefore, the length is 168m³ ÷ (8m × 7m) = 168m³ ÷ 56m² = **3m**.
13	17.5m²	Volume of cuboid = length × height × width Therefore, the height is 140m³ ÷ (8m × 5m) = 140m³ ÷ 40m² = 3.5m. Therefore, the area of face A is 3.5m × 5m = **17.5m²**.
14	51.2m³	Volume of cylindrical swimming pool = area of circular end × height 32m² × 1.6m = **51.2m³**
15	162cm³	IXcm = 9cm, IIIcm = 3cm, VIcm = 6cm Therefore, the volume is 9cm × 3cm × 6cm = **162cm³**.

3D Shapes and Volumes - Advanced, page 48

Question	Answer	Explanation
1	98	3 tetrahedrons: 3 × 6 = 18 edges. 3 octagonal prisms: 3 × 24 = 72 edges. 1 square-based pyramid: 8 edges. Therefore, the total number of edges is 18 + 72 + 8 = **98**.
2	2,880°	A pentagonal prism is comprised of 5 rectangles and 2 pentagons. The sum of the interior angles in a rectangle is 360° and the sum of the interior angles in a pentagon is 540°. Therefore, the sum of the interior angles on all of the faces is (5 × 360°) + (2 × 540°) = 1,800° + 1,080° = **2,880°**.
3	7.67	The shapes have the following number of vertices; hexagonal prism (12), triangular prism (6), pentagonal prism (10), cube (8), tetrahedron (4) and triangular wedge (6). The mean number of vertices is (12 + 6 + 10 + 8 + 4 + 6) ÷ 6 = **7.67**.
4	$x(yz + 3x + 1)$	Volume of cuboid A = xyz. Volume of cuboid B = $(x - 1)x$. Volume of cuboid C = $2x(x + 1)$. The combined volume of cuboids A, B and C is $xyz + x(x - 1) + 2x(x + 1) = x(yz + (x - 1) + 2(x + 1)) = x(yz + x - 1 + 2x + 2) = \mathbf{x(yz + 3x + 1)}$.
5	4	A cuboid has 12 edges, a triangular prism has 9 (square number), a tetrahedron has 6, a pentagonal prism has 15, a square-based pyramid has 8 (cube number) and an octahedron has 12. **4** of the 6 shapes do not have a square or cube number of edges.
6	13.6m³	Volume of pool above water = length × height × width = 8m × 0.5m × 4.5m = 18m³. Volume of water in pool = 31.6m³ − 18m³ = **13.6m³**.
7	56.16cm³	1.8cm × 0.052m × 60mm = 1.8cm × 5.2cm × 6cm = **56.16cm³**
8	2744cm³	If the perimeter of two faces on a cube is 112cm, the perimeter of one face is 112cm ÷ 2 = 56cm. Therefore, the side length must be 56cm ÷ 4 = 14cm. Therefore, the volume is 14cm × 14cm × 14cm = **2744cm³**.
9	286	Volume of box = 11cm × 7cm × 6.5cm = 500.5cm³. Volume of sphere is 1.75cm³. Volume of the box is 500.5cm³ ÷ 1.75cm³ = **286** times larger than the volume of the sphere.
10	228cm³	The shape can be split into two cuboids. Volume of shorter cuboid: 5cm × 4cm × 3cm = 60cm³. Volume of longer cuboid: (5cm + 5cm + 4cm) × 4cm × 3cm = 14cm × 4cm × 3cm = 168cm³. Therefore, the volume of the whole shape is 60cm³ + 168cm³ = **228cm³**.
11	113.52cm³	24 cubes make up the cuboid. Each cube has a volume of 4.73cm³. Therefore, the volume of the cuboid is 24 × 4.73cm³ = **113.52cm³**.
12	213.3cm³	(32.9cm³ × 3) + (19.1cm³ × 6) = 98.7cm³ + 114.6cm³ = **213.3cm³**
13	4,608cm³	Area of trapezium = $\frac{1}{2} \times h \times (a + b)$ (where a and b are the parallel sides and h is the perpendicular height) = ½ × 8cm × (12cm + (6cm + 12cm + 6cm)) = ½ × 8cm × 36cm = 144cm². Volume of ingot = area of trapezium × length = 144cm² × 32cm = **4,608cm³**.
14	XLmm	Width is 256cm³ ÷ (4cm × 16cm) = 256cm³ ÷ 64cm² = 4cm = 40mm = **XLmm**.
15	3499.2cm³	Width = 4.5 × 12cm = 54cm. Height = $^{45}/_{100}$ × 12cm = 5.4cm. Volume of cuboid = 12cm × 5.4cm × 54cm = **3499.2cm³**.

Probability - Beginner, page 50

Question	Answer	Explanation
1	certain	It is **certain** that the month of August directly follows the month of July.
2	even chance	There are 6 different outcomes (1, 2, 3, 4, 5 or 6) when rolling a fair die. An even chance is when there is a 50% chance of an event occurring. Therefore, there is an **even chance** of the die landing on 4, 5 or 6.
3	unlikely	It is **unlikely** it will snow for 20 days in a row in London.
4	likely	It is **likely** that the temperature will reach 25°C on at least one day in August in England.
5	impossible	It is **impossible** for a square to have 5 sides.
6	$1/3$	There are 6 numbers and 2 of them are greater than 6 (9 and 10). Therefore, the probability of the number being greater than 6 is $2/6 = \mathbf{1/3}$.
7	0.5	P(not heads) = P(tails) = $1/2$ = **0.5**.
8	$1/2$	There are 6 sections on the spinner, 1 is black, 2 are grey and 3 are white. Therefore, the probability of the spinner landing on a white section = $3/6 = \mathbf{1/2}$.
9	0	It is impossible for tomorrow to be the 8th January if today is the 4th January. Tomorrow would be the 5th January.
10	$1/6$	1 face on a die contains an odd number which is not 1 or 3 (5). As a fraction of the 6 faces, this is $\mathbf{1/6}$.
11	$2/5$	4 of the 10 discs have a 4 on them. Therefore, the probability of selecting a disc with a 4 is $4/10 = \mathbf{2/5}$.
12	$3/4$	25% of the pencils are broken. Therefore, 75% of the pencils are not broken, which as a fraction is $75/100 = \mathbf{3/4}$.
13	$2/7$	2 of the 7 letters are As, which as a fraction is $\mathbf{2/7}$.
14	$1/4$	13 of the 52 cards in a standard pack of playing cards are from the hearts suit, which as a fraction is $13/52 = \mathbf{1/4}$.
15	$2/3$	8 of the 12 squares are shaded, which as a fraction is $8/12 = \mathbf{2/3}$.

Probability - Intermediate, page 51

Question	Answer	Explanation
1	likely	3 of the 4 subjects contain the letter 'o' (history, sociology and computing). Therefore, it is **likely** that a subject chosen will contain the letter 'o'.
2	unlikely	It is **unlikely** that heads will not occur at all when tossing a fair coin 10 times.
3	certain	If today is Monday 14th, it is **certain** that last Monday was the 7th and one week from tomorrow, it will be the 22nd.
4	even chance	4 of the 8 notes are worth more than £10. An even chance is when there is a 50% chance of an event occurring. Therefore, there is an **even chance** ($4/8$) that a note chosen at random is worth more than £10.
5	impossible	It is **impossible** that the pm part of a day is 730 minutes as it lasts for 12 × 60 minutes = 720 minutes.
6	$1/6$	2 of the 12 discs (36 and 42) have numbers on them which are exactly divisible by 2 and 3. Therefore, the probability of selecting one of these discs is $2/12 = 1/6$.
7	$3/26$	There are 26 black cards in a pack of 52 playing cards. Of the 26 black cards there are 2 aces, 2 threes and 2 queens, making a total of 6 cards, which as a fraction of all cards is $6/52 = 3/26$.
8	18 days	40 days × 45% = 40 days × $45/100$ = **18 days**
9	$3/5$	The box consists of 3 + 5 + 12 = 20 coins in total. 12 of these coins are circular, which as a fraction of all coins is $12/20 = 3/5$.
10	$5/16$	There are test marks for 2 + 8 + 10 + 9 + 3 = 32 students in total. 10 of these scored between 10 and 30, which as a fraction is $10/32 = 5/16$.
11	$5/12$	5 of the 12 months in a year have less than 31 days (February, April, June, September and November), which as a fraction is $5/12$.
12	$6/25$	Number of squares: 5 × 5 = 25. 6 squares contain triangular numbers (1, 3, 6, 10, 15 and 21), which as a fraction is $6/25$.
13	$1/3$	2 of the 6 faces on a die contain numbers 2 and 6 (which are the equivalent of Roman numerals II and VI respectively). As a fraction of the 6 faces this is $2/6 = 1/3$.
14	$7/20$	Number of squares: 8 × 5 = 40. 14 squares contain a smiley face, which as a fraction is $14/40 = 7/20$.
15	$2/3$	Of the 6 faces on the spinner, 4 have numbers on them which are greater than 3. As a fraction, this is $4/6 = 2/3$.

Probability - Advanced, page 52

Question	Answer	Explanation
1	$1/64$	P(all 6 coins show heads) = $1/2 \times 1/2 \times 1/2 \times 1/2 \times 1/2 \times 1/2$ = $\mathbf{1/64}$.
2	45%	The room contains 174 + 360 + 38 + 209 + 19 = 800 objects in total. 360 of these objects are print cartridges, which as a percentage is $360/800 \times 100$ = **45%**.
3	$25/64$	Left spinner: P(cube number) = $5/8$. Right spinner: P(number > 9.76) = $5/8$. Therefore, the probability that both occur is $5/8 \times 5/8$ = $\mathbf{25/64}$.
4	$1/4$	After adding the 4 cards, there are 56 in total. 14 are black and have a value between 3 and 8. Therefore, P (black and have a value between 3 and 8) = $14/56$ = $\mathbf{1/4}$.
5	33	Expected number of green chairs with 4 legs: $15 \times 2/5$ = 6. Expected number of green chairs with 3 legs: $18 \times 1/6$ = 3. Therefore, the number of legs on these chairs is $(6 \times 4) + (3 \times 3)$ = 24 + 9 = **33**.
6	138	P (less than 5) = P (1 or 2 or 3 or 4) = $4/6 \times 207$ = $2/3 \times 207$ = **138**.
7	$13/147$	The total number of vehicles is 78 + 18 + 9 + 16 + 5 = 126. The probability of selecting a car followed by a van (with replacement) is $78/126 \times 18/126$ = $13/21 \times 1/7$ = $\mathbf{13/147}$.
8	$2/5$	Mean score per ball = Sum of scores ÷ Amount of balls. Sum of scores is given by: $(3 \times 16) + (8 \times 23) + (4 \times 13) + (5 \times 14)$ = 48 + 184 + 52 + 70 = 354 points. Therefore, the mean score per ball = 354 points ÷ 20 balls = 17.7 points per ball. P (ball selected at random is worth more than 17.7 points) = $8/20$ = $\mathbf{2/5}$.
9	$7/15$	P(loss) = $1 - (2/15 + 2/5)$ = $1 - (2/15 + 6/15)$ = $1 - 8/15$ = $\mathbf{7/15}$.
10	$52/125$	Left box: P(shaded ball) = $20/25$ = $4/5$. Right box: P(shaded ball) = $13/25$. Therefore, the probability that both balls are shaded is $4/5 \times 13/25$ = $\mathbf{52/125}$.
11	$5/8$	There are 8 sections on the spinner, 2 are grey and 3 are black. Therefore, the probability of landing on black or grey is $(2+3)/8$ = $\mathbf{5/8}$.
12	$1/56$	P(LLL) = $3/8 \times 2/7 \times 1/6$ = $\mathbf{1/56}$.
13	$2/9$	First die: P(throwing a number ≤ 2) = $2/6$ = $1/3$. Second die: P(throwing a number ≥ 3) = $4/6$ = $2/3$. Therefore, the probability that both occur is $1/3 \times 2/3$ = $\mathbf{2/9}$.
14	63	P(selecting a blue paper clip) = 100% − (22% + 36%) = 42%. Therefore, the number of blue paper clips is $150 \times 42\%$ = 150×0.42 = **63**.
15	$1/4$	P(tail) = $1/2$. P(even number) = $3/6$ = $1/2$. Therefore, the probability is $1/2 \times 1/2$ = $\mathbf{1/4}$.

Coordinates and Transformations - Beginner, page 54

Question	Answer	Explanation
1	**(4, 2)**	x-coordinate: (2 + 6) ÷ 2 = 8 ÷ 2 = 4. y-coordinate: (2 + 2) ÷ 2 = 4 ÷ 2 = 2. Therefore, the coordinates of the midpoint are **(4, 2)**.
2	**(2, 5)**	Point K is at coordinates **(2, 5)**.
3	**(5, 3)**	The centre of the circle is at coordinates **(5, 3)**.
4	**(1, 5)**	The coordinates of the last corner of the rectangle are **(1, 5)**.
5	**yes**	The straight line passing through (−2, −2), (1, 1) and (5, 5) will also pass through (0, 0). **Yes**
6	**rhombus**	The coordinates (4, 6), (5, 4), (4, 2) and (3, 4) form a **rhombus**.
7	**(10, 0)**	The treasure is at coordinates **(10, 0)**.
8	**(0, 2)**	Point A at coordinates (0, 4) is translated 2 units down to its new position of **(0, 2)**.
9	**(3, 4)**	The museum at coordinates (6, 3) is translated three units left, then one unit up to its new position of **(3, 4)**.
10	**(5, 1)**	Point P at coordinates (1, 3) is translated four units right, then two units down to its new position of **(5, 1)**.
11	**(1, 3)**	Point B at coordinates (−1, 3) is reflected in the y-axis, taking it to point **(1, 3)**.
12	**(2, 4)**	Point C at coordinates (4, 4) is reflected in the line x = 3, taking it to point **(2, 4)**.
13	**(3, 2)**	After the two transformations, the new coordinates of point H are **(3, 2)**.
14	**(1, 0)**	Point W at coordinates (0, 1) is rotated 90° clockwise about the origin to its new position of **(1, 0)**.
15	**B**	Diagram **B** shows the line rotated 180° anticlockwise about its centre.

Coordinates and Transformations - Intermediate, page 55

Question	Answer	Explanation
1	(−0.5, 7)	x-coordinate: (−5 + 4) ÷ 2 = −1 ÷ 2 = −0.5. y-coordinate: (7 + 7) ÷ 2 = 14 ÷ 2 = 7. Therefore, the coordinates of the midpoint are **(−0.5, 7)**.
2	E	Point **E** is at coordinates (−3, 2).
3	(−2, 0)	The coordinates of the last corner of the parallelogram are **(−2, 0)**.
4	(−6, −3)	The chemist is at coordinates **(−6, −3)**.
5	(4, −2)	The length of each side of the square is 6 units. Therefore, the centre coordinates are 3 units in from each set of corner coordinates. The centre is therefore at coordinates **(4, −2)**.
6	(8, 6)	Length b on the triangle looking at the y-coordinates 6 − 1 = 5. Therefore, the coordinates of point Q must be (3 + 5, 6) = **(8, 6)**.
7	(5, −4)	Point G at coordinates (0, 2) is translated three units down, then five units right and lastly 3 units down to its new position of **(5, −4)**.
8	(−9, 20)	Point V is at coordinates (−13 + 4, 14) = (−9, 14). It is translated 6 units up, which takes it to coordinates (−9, 14 + 6) = **(−9, 20)**.
9	(50, −40)	The point which is directly east of point S at (−40, −40) is point T at **(50, −40)**.
10	(−15.45, 2)	Point P at coordinates (−2, 2) is translated 13.45 units left to its new position of **(−15.45, 2)**.
11	(−0.5, −0.17)	Point Q at coordinates (0.5, −0.17) is reflected in the y-axis, taking it to point **(−0.5, −0.17)**.
12	(7, 3)	Point C at coordinates (2, 3) is reflected in line M at x = 4.5, taking it to point **(7, 3)**.
13	L4	Point P must be reflected in line **L4** to move it to point Q.
14	(−3, 1)	Point R at coordinates (−1, −3) is rotated 90° clockwise about the origin to its new position of **(−3, 1)**.
15	(1, −1)	Point Z at coordinates (1, 1) is rotated three right angles (3 × 90° = 270°) anticlockwise about the origin to its new position of **(1, −1)**.

Coordinates and Transformations - Advanced, page 56

Question	Answer	Explanation
1	(−5, −2)	The point which is directly northwest of the hospital at $(-\sqrt{9}, -(2^2)) = (-3, -4)$ is point A at **(−5, −2)**.
2	5 points	Harin scores the following points: 1 at (2, 0), −1 at (−4, 1), 2 at (−5, 3), −2 at (3, 3), 1 at (2, 0) and 4 at (1, 4). Therefore, this makes a total of 1 − 1 + 2 − 2 + 1 + 4 = **5 points**.
3	(3, 3)	After the three transformations, the new coordinates for point A are **(3, 3)**.
4	(−16, 6)	After the two transformations, the new coordinates for point Z are **(−16, 6)**.
5	(−0.93, −0.84)	Point J at coordinates (0.63, 0.09) is translated 1.56 units left and then 0.93 units down to its new position at **(−0.93, −0.84)**.
6	(0, 5) and (10, 5) or (0, −5) and (10, −5)	The area of the rectangle is 50cm^2. Its length is 10cm − 0cm = 10cm. Height of rectangle = area ÷ length = 50cm^2 ÷ 10cm = 5cm. The possible coordinates of the remaining corner coordinates are (0, 0 + 5) and (10, 0 + 5) or (0, 0 − 5) and (10, 0 − 5) = **(0, 5) and (10, 5)** or **(0, −5) and (10, −5)**.
7	(5, 7)	Point C at coordinates $(2 + 1^4, \sqrt{49}) = (2 + 1, 7) = (3, 7)$ is reflected in the line $x = 4$, taking it to point **(5, 7)**.
8	(6, −3)	Point A at coordinates (4, 1) is rotated 90° clockwise about (3, −2) to its new position of **(6, −3)**.
9	(−1, −2)	After the two transformations, the only point where the two shapes touch is at **(−1, −2)**.
10	(2.5, −3)	After the rectangle is reflected in the dashed line its centre coordinates are at **(2.5, −3)**.
11	$\begin{pmatrix} -0.5 \\ -4.5 \end{pmatrix}$	Point A at coordinates (4, 1) needs to be translated left 0.5 units and down 4.5 units to map it onto the centre coordinates of the circle at (3.5, −3.5). Therefore, the translation is $\begin{pmatrix} -0.5 \\ -4.5 \end{pmatrix}$.
12	(−25, −20)	After the two transformations, the new coordinates that Jan is standing at are **(−25, −20)**.
13	(−2, −5)	After the three transformations, the new coordinates for point M are **(−2, −5)**.
14	£8.36	Miss Smith finds the following amounts of money: £2.40 at (−8, 0), £4.24 at (4, 10), £1.17 at (−6, 4) and £0.55 at (−8, 8). Therefore, this makes a total of £2.40 + £4.24 + £1.17 + £0.55 = **£8.36**.
15	(−1.65, 0.75)	After the two transformations, the new coordinates for point N are **(−1.65, 0.75)**.

Other Titles in the First Past The Post® Series

Mathematics: Dictionary Plus

This book is an indispensable companion to our practice papers and workbooks, containing definitions of key mathematical concepts in accessible language. Each definition is accompanied by a worked, illustrated example and a series of questions to ensure a thorough understanding of its practical applications. The questions have two tiers of difficulty: 'Test yourself' and 'Challenge yourself'. Full answers are included.

This is a comprehensive reference volume, invaluable for all students at 11 plus and Common Entrance exams, Key Stage 2 and beyond.